AUSTRALIAN BUSHRANGERS

Robert Coupe

First published in Australia in 1998 and reprinted in 2007 and 2009
New Holland Publishers (Australia) Pty Ltd
Sydney • Auckland • London • Cape Town

Produced and published in Australia by
New Holland Publishers (Australia) Pty Ltd
1/66 Gibbes Street Chatswood NSW 2067 Australia
218 Lake Road Northcote Auckland New Zealand
86 Edgware Road London W2 2EA United Kingdom
80 McKenzie Street Cape Town 8001 South Africa

Copyright © 1998 in text: Robert Coupe
Copyright © 1998 in maps: Dizign
Copyright © 1998 in pictures: as indicated below

All rights reserved. No part of this publication may be reproduced, stored in a retrieval system or transmitted, in any form or by any means, electronic, mechanical, photocopying, recording or otherwise, without the prior written permission of the publishers and copyright holders.

Editor: Anna Saunders
Designer: Tricia McCallum
Typesetter: Midland Typesetters
Manufactured in China by Jade Productions

National Library of Australia Cataloguing-in-Publication Data:

>   Coupe, Robert.
>   Australian bushrangers
>
>   Includes index.
>   ISBN 9781741106732.
>
>   1. Bushrangers—Australia. I. Title
>
>   364.1550994

All pictures from the National Library of Australia with the exception of the following:

Shaen Adey/New Holland Image Library: front cover top; Getty: front cover top right; Archives Office of Tasmania: p.14; Reproduced with the permission of the Keeper of Public Records, Victoria (Citation; PROV, VPR515/P, unit 17 page 287 # 10926): p. 170; Image Library, State Library of New South Wales: p. 53; La Trobe Picture Collection, State Library of Victoria: p. 58–59, 188–189, 190–191; Courtesy of Victoria Police Historical Unit: p. 117.

CONTENTS

EARLY DAYS
The Beginnings of Australian Bushranging 1

THE EARLY VANDEMONIANS
Gentlemen and Cannibals 4

MATTHEW BRADY
A Popular Hero 15

MARTIN CASH
From Outlaw to Landowner 25

EARLY MAINLAND BUSHRANGERS
Wild Colonial Boys 40

THE EUREKA GANG AND CAPTAIN MELVILLE
Bushrangers of the Victorian Goldfields 62

FRANK GARDINER
New Outbreaks in New South Wales 72

BEN HALL
A Man of High Renown 87

'MAD DAN' MORGAN
A Cold-blooded Killer 106

THOMAS AND JOHN CLARKE
Brothers-in-arms 119

FREDERICK WARD
A Self-styled Thunderbolt 127

CAPTAIN MOONLITE
A Master Trickster 139

JAMES MCPHERSON
The Elusive 'Wild Scotchman' 149

HARRY POWER
A Victim of Betrayal 159

THE KELLY GANG
Everlasting Folk Heroes 165

Index 193

EARLY DAYS
The Beginnings of Australian Bushranging

An aura of romance surrounds the idea of Australian bushrangers. The passage of time has invested the most celebrated of them—the Ben Halls and the members of the Kelly gang—with a kind of swashbuckling dash; they are often portrayed as men who pitted their wits and skills against the dangers and privations of life on the run and the superior resources of an unjust and oppressive regime.

Bushranging was a feature of Australian existence for almost a century—from the founding of a British penal colony on the shores of Port Jackson in 1788 to the execution of Ned Kelly in Melbourne gaol in November 1880. But it was not a continuous or a widespread phenomenon; it was largely confined to the south-eastern part of the continent and the island of Tasmania, and erupted spasmodically in a number of phases.

Australian bushranging was an inevitable outcome of the conditions under which the colony of New South Wales was settled. The settlement of about 1500 people that was established at Sydney Cove on 26 January 1788 consisted about half of convicts who had been transported for crimes ranging from petty theft to highway robbery, and the rest of officials, soldiers and guards. In the open prison that was early Sydney, it was inevitable that many of these unwilling settlers would take the ample opportunities that presented themselves to abscond and try their luck in the seemingly limitless bush that surrounded the settlement. Very few of the convicts had any education to speak of and no-one had any knowledge of the country's geography. Some, it seemed, imagined that by making their way inland they would find a way to China.

These early 'bolters', as they became known, were a far cry from any ideal

Convicts line up outside Sydney's Hyde Park Barracks to work in a road gang. Many such men took the opportunity to 'bolt' and try their luck in the bush.

of romance or heroism. They were bushrangers only in the sense that they ranged about the bush, exploiting its meagre resources in order to survive. A number of them perished from hunger and exposure or were speared by Aboriginal people; many more returned to accept the 50 or more lashes that were routinely meted out to such absconders.

The first of these bushrangers to make any lasting impression on the colony was a Negro called John Caesar. Caesar was an imposing figure with a powerful physique. He had been a slave on a West Indian plantation, but had contrived to stow away on a British ship. He made his way to London where he took to petty theft. He was caught, convicted and sentenced to seven years' transportation to Botany Bay. He arrived on the First Fleet.

In his first year in the colony, Caesar, who was widely known as 'Black Caesar', was convicted of stealing food and given a punishment of 500 lashes.

In June 1789 he again stole some food, but this time escaped into the bush in an attempt to avoid punishment. Here he was attacked by hostile Aboriginal people and returned and surrendered to the authorities. This time he was sentenced to a term on Norfolk Island, the convict settlement that had been established far out in the South Pacific to accommodate convicts who had committed offences after arriving in the colony. It was termed, in the euphemistic officialese of the time, a place of 'secondary punishment', where inmates were subjected to a regime of grim brutality.

When he had served his sentence there, Caesar returned to Sydney where he promptly escaped once again into the bush, only to be quickly recaptured and once again flogged. Caesar absconded yet again and this time led a gang of other escaped convicts who carried out raids on the properties of settlers which by this time were spreading out westwards from the original settlement. The governor, John Hunter, placed a bounty of five gallons (about 23 litres) of rum on Caesar's head and in 1796 he was hunted down and shot dead at Liberty Plains, near the present suburb of Burwood in Sydney's west.

John Caesar was, by any account, a minor figure in the pantheon of Australian bushrangers. But he set the pattern for future practitioners of the craft, first by being the leader of a marauding gang and, second, by having a price put upon his head. He is also the first in a more or less distinguished line to have fallen prey to a bounty hunter.

THE EARLY VANDEMONIANS
Gentlemen and Cannibals

The first serious outbreaks of bushranging in Australia occurred, not in Sydney, but in Tasmania, which was then known as Van Diemen's Land. Conditions there were even more conducive to a state of disorder than they were in Sydney. For 20 years after the first convict settlement was established on the banks of the Derwent River in 1803, Van Diemen's Land received only prisoners who had been reconvicted since their arrival in New South Wales. It was, then, like Norfolk Island, a place of secondary punishment and contained many of the most hardened and desperate criminals in the colony. With such a population, Hobart Town, as the young settlement was known, was a forbidding place.

The feeling of alienation was further heightened when, in 1805, expected shipments of food and other stores failed to materialise and the settlement's population was threatened with starvation.

In these circumstances, the lieutenant governor, David Collins, had little alternative but to issue guns to the men—soldiers, settlers and convicts alike—with orders to go out into the bush and hunt the kangaroos that abounded there. It was not long before this abundance of kangaroos was reduced to a dearth in the immediate environs of Hobart and the hunters were forced further out from the settled areas and ever deeper into the hinterland. Armed, then, with the means both of survival and defence, it is not surprising that many convicts chose to escape.

Escape and survival became easier as time went on and sheep runs and other settlements were established further out from both Hobart and the smaller settlement that had been established in 1804 at Port Dalrymple, on the island's north coast. Most of the absconders operated alone and subsisted by sheep stealing and other petty theft, although desperation led some to commit violence against or even murder outlying settlers or others of their kind. Occasionally these men lived and hunted in groups of two or three. In the more remote locations the escapees were able to trade kangaroo meat and skins—as well as sheep that they had stolen from other settlers—for ammunition and other supplies. The outlying settlers were understandably nervous about these free-ranging bandits and were keen not to antagonise them and thus invite reprisals.

Lieutenant Governor David Collins

Lemon's gang

A notorious group of three operated in the Oyster Bay area, south of Hobart, from about 1805. It consisted of an Englishman, Richard Lemon, and two Irishmen named Scanlon and Brown. They were a rough and ruthless trio who were noted for their brutal treatment of Aboriginal people. They had no compunction about using the natives for recreational target practice.

Internal dissension soon spelt the beginning of the end for this small murderous gang. Scanlon and Brown infuriated Lemon by their habit of talking to each other in Gaelic, which he could not understand. One day when Brown was away from their camp, Lemon casually shot Scanlon dead. Despite the loss of his fellow compatriot, Brown stayed with Lemon and the two carried on their murderous escapades for another two years. Eventually they were tracked down and taken prisoner by a group of convict bounty hunters. No less ruthless than their captives, the convicts shot Lemon dead and ordered Brown to chop off his head and carry it back with them to Hobart. One live prisoner and evidence that the other was dead was sufficient to secure the convicts their unconditional release.

Whitehead's brutality

David Collins died suddenly in 1810 and was replaced as lieutenant governor of Van Diemen's Land by Thomas Davey. Davey's period of office was marked by a veritable epidemic of bushranging. Most bushrangers still operated singly or in very small groups, but a number of larger gangs also began to emerge. One such gang was led by an escaped convict named Whitehead. By September 1810 this gang had acquired such a reputation for pillaging the farms of settlers near Hobart that the new lieutenant governor placed a notice in the *Hobart Town*

Gazette offering rewards for the capture of its leader or other members. Whitehead was merciless to those he suspected, with or without justification, of being his enemies. He is reported to have murdered one unfortunate suspect whom the gang tortured by placing bull ants in a pair of leather moccasins and attaching them to the victim's feet. The gang, however, continued to thrive, and by 1814 it included among its numbers a 27-year-old desperado called Michael Howe.

Howe had what seemed like a perfect pedigree for a bushranger—he had been transported to Sydney for highway robbery, and also had a history of deserting from both the merchant navy and the army. He reoffended in Sydney and was sent to Hobart, where he arrived in 1812. His chronic insubordination brought harsh punishments, including numerous floggings. However, he did not remain long in custody. He soon made his escape and by 1814 was one of the 28 members of Whitehead's gang. By this time the gang was greatly feared, especially in the area around New Norfolk, where they preyed particularly on the properties of settlers who were known to mistreat convicts. One magistrate who was notorious for ordering brutal floggings had his sheep stolen, his crops burnt and his house vandalised by Whitehead and his gang.

At this time Van Diemen's Land was still part of the colony of New South Wales, which by now was under the governorship of Lachlan Macquarie. So concerned was Macquarie by what seemed like a state of anarchy in Van Diemen's Land that he ordered Davey to make a proclamation offering a pardon to any bushranger who surrendered before 1 December 1814. The response was an upsurge, rather than a diminution, in bushranging activity. Davey's answer was to hang as many apprehended absconders as possible and to allow their bodies to slowly rot away in public view as a grisly deterrent to any who might follow their example.

A leader of panache and style

In October 1814 some soldiers came upon Whitehead in the area around Launceston and shot him dead. Howe was elected as the new leader and soon imposed his own distinctive, if rather bizarre and brutal, leadership style. He made his underlings swear their allegiance on a prayer book and kept a diary bound in kangaroo skin in which he wrote in blood. There was more than a streak of megalomania in Howe's make-up and he was convinced that destiny had singled him out as a kind of avenging angel who would wreak retribution on the oppressive authorities. Despite this, he was prepared to deal with these authorities, although very much on his own terms.

In 1816 he sent, via an intermediary, a peremptorily worded letter to Davey, in which he indignantly denied the charges of brutality that had been made against his gang, protesting that they resorted to violence only when circumstances forced them to. Davey accepted the letter from Howe's messenger, a whaler named Westlick, and sent back a surprisingly conciliatory message, claiming, perhaps a little too disingenuously, that if Howe and his men forsook their present course and returned to Hobart, no harm would befall them. Not surprisingly, Howe did not take the lieutenant governor at his word, but continued his marauding ways.

By this time Howe, who was generally known as 'Mike' Howe and whose panache and style had inspired a degree of popular admiration, was ranging widely through what is now central Tasmania, from near Launceston in the north to Hobart. His protestations of non-violence are hardly borne out by the facts. On one occasion Howe led a murderous attack on a group of Aboriginal people, abducting a number of the women to serve as wives for himself and his comrades. This raid has been seen by some as the catalyst for the ensuing hostilities between blacks and whites which ended so catastrophically for Tasmania's Aboriginal people.

Despite the manner in which she had been seized, Howe's Aboriginal 'wife', known as 'Black Mary', remained with him and is credited with using her understanding of the bush to help him escape several times from bands of soldiers who were sent out to hunt him.

In 1817 Thomas Davey was replaced as lieutenant governor of Van Diemen's Land by Colonel William Sorell. Soon after Sorell's arrival, Howe came very close to being captured when he and Black Mary were ambushed by soldiers. Howe, who was fleet of foot, managed to escape arrest but in the exchange of fire he, probably accidentally, shot Mary, who was heavily pregnant and unable to keep up. Howe made good his escape, unheroically leaving Mary to the mercy of her captors.

Mary recovered from her wound and gave birth to Howe's child. Then, perhaps believing the official 'line' put about by the authorities that Howe had attempted to murder her, she agreed to guide search parties in pursuit of him. She did not succeed, but by this time Howe was beginning to feel the heat. He once again communicated with the authorities, this time sending a letter to Sorell.

If Howe was feeling insecure, the tone of his letter belied this. Pretending to an equal status with the lieutenant governor, Howe addressed his letter with typical bravado to the 'lieutenant governor of the town' from the 'lieutenant governor of the woods'. In it he set out, effectively, his terms of surrender. He would give himself up and forgo his previous way of life on condition that he be let go free. That such a preposterously arrogant proposal was even considered is an indication of the grudging esteem in which, even at an official level, he was held. Sorell, perhaps keen to end the Howe problem once and for all, sent an emissary to meet the bushranger. Howe returned to Hobart where he was allowed to roam free pending Sorell's written request to Governor Macquarie that he receive a free pardon. In the meantime, Howe began to inform, not only on the members of his gang, but also on settlers who had collaborated with them by, for example, receiving stolen goods.

Howe's attempts to ingratiate himself with the powers that be produced no immediate results. The sense of security that his freedom in the town gave him was supplanted by a suspicion that arrest and condemnation were imminent. In September 1817 he absconded for the last time. His gang members no longer felt they could trust him and in any case the gang had broken up into smaller groups. Howe, now left to his own resources, made for the Central Highlands where for some time he survived by terrorising and robbing remote settlers. With a price of £100 on his head, he was now prey to bounty hunters. On one occasion two former convicts managed to capture the sleeping Howe, who, nevertheless, managed to break loose. killing one of his captors and wounding the other.

Late in 1818 the inevitable end arrived. A soldier named William Pugh and a sailor named John Worral tracked him to his mountain camp on the Shannon River. Worral and Howe confronted each other with guns; Howe's shot missed and Worral's hit the mark. Pugh then finished off his quarry by battering him about the head. As proof of their achievement the two bounty hunters carried Howe's head back to Hobart and delivered it to Sorell, who had it displayed publicly.

Howe's demise did not, as was hoped, spell an end to the rash of absconders-turned-bushrangers in Van Diemen's Land. Nor did the draconian punishments meted out to those unfortunate enough to be caught. At least 19 bushrangers were hanged in Hobart and Launceston in 1821 and, despite an optimistic assessment by Governor Macquarie that the problem was now at an end, the depredations continued unabated.

Macquarie Harbour

Hobart, now the capital of the state of Tasmania, was founded as a place of secondary punishment. In 1823 the settlement on the Derwent received its first consignment of convicts who were newly arrived in the colony. However, continuing the tradition of using the island as a dumping ground for unregenerates, a new penal settlement had been opened in January of the previous year at Macquarie Harbour on the rugged south-west of the island. It was a forbidding place. Covering almost 300 square kilometres, Macquarie Harbour is one of the world's largest natural harbours. The treacherous, shallow entrance to it is through a pair of headlands dubbed by convicts 'Hell's Gates', both for the dangers inherent in passing through them and for the grimness of what lay beyond. The convicts were housed on two islands within the harbour. Most lived on Sarah Island, the larger of the two, but the most hardened were confined to a two-room building on the tiny nearby Grummet Island which soon acquired the sombre nickname the 'Isle of the Condemned'.

Macquarie Harbour had both the advantage and disadvantage of being remote. Its isolation made escape, if not difficult, at least extremely hazardous. Thick forests and almost impenetrable craggy mountains separated it from settlements to the north and east, and escape by sea involved even greater dangers. Macquarie Harbour's relative inaccessibility also meant that supplies, other than those that could be obtained or grown on the spot, were often scarce. Scurvy, a disease that resulted mainly from a lack of vitamin C and that afflicted many of Australia's early explorers, was common among convicts.

Convicts at Macquarie Harbour worked in a number of enterprises, including boatbuilding, small-scale farming, tanning and timber-getting. The shores of the harbour were thickly wooded and the much sought-after Huon pine was abundant in the area. Many of the convicts spent their time in the dangerous and back-breaking task of felling and transporting these forest giants. A number of convicts were killed in logging accidents. Many seized the opportunity presented by this work to abscond into the bush. In the first two years of the settlement it has been estimated that about 10 per cent of the convict population escaped and attempted to find their way to the more hospitable country to the east. Of those that remained at large, few were ever heard of again.

Cannibals in the bush

One of the earliest, and probably the most notorious, of the escapees from Macquarie Harbour was an Irishman named Alexander Pearce. He was the only inmate of Macquarie Harbour to escape twice. The 30-year-old Pearce arrived in Hobart in 1820 to serve a seven-year sentence for stealing shoes. He was soon in trouble, both as a chronic absconder and a thief and, despite numerous floggings, he persisted in his ways. In 1822 he was sent to Macquarie Harbour where he was put to work in the sawpits on Sarah Island. On 20 September in that year Pearce and six others stole a rowboat and made for the shore. Here they destroyed the boat, picked up an eighth man, Robert Greenhill and, armed with axes and whatever food they could gather, set off through the forest, heading east in the direction of Hobart.

Pearce had learned some bushcraft and survival skills in several of his previous fairly extended spells of illegal freedom. But he and his companions were not prepared for the rigours of the countryside into which they were now venturing. For more than three months the gang made their way, in ever-decreasing numbers, through the thick, wet forests and over successive ranges of hills and mountains, until in January 1823, Pearce, the last surviving member, was arrested by soldiers in the vicinity of Hobart. Pearce has left his own account of his bizarre and horrifying odyssey in a confession which he dictated to the authorities in Hobart.

Within a week of their escape, the gang's provisions had run out, the weather had turned cold and wet, and desperation, born of hunger and weakness, set in. According to Pearce's confession, the first intimations of the horrors to follow came from William Kennelly, known to his companions as Bill Cornelius, who claimed to be so hungry that he could 'eat a piece of a man'. The idea took root, with Bob Greenhill claiming some experience of eating human flesh and saying it tasted 'much like pork'. The next night Greenhill slew Alexander Dalton with his axe as he lay asleep. Greenhill justified the murder on the grounds, probably spurious, that Dalton had volunteered to be a flogger. Dalton's body was dismembered and the flesh divided up among the seven remaining men.

Not long after this, Kennelly and another man, known as 'Little' Brown, fearful for their lives, quietly absconded from the gang to make their way back to Macquarie Harbour. In mid-October they were found more dead than alive near the settlement, still carrying some of Dalton's remains. Both of them died within days of their recapture from the effects of their ordeal.

The five survivors, now consumed with mutual suspicion and dread, reached and crossed the Franklin River, and were soon again racked with hunger. Four of them decided that Thomas Bodenham, who had been convicted for highway robbery, should be the next victim, and he was duly slain by Greenhill, who by this time was in possession of the only remaining axe.

Ironically, they had now reached country that abounded with kangaroos, emus and other game, but with only one axe between them they had no means of hunting them. They could prey only on their own kind and John Mather, a Scotsman who had been unable to stomach Bodenham's flesh, was the next to be slaughtered by Greenhill's axe. Mather's death had something of the grotesque ritual of a formal execution. When Greenhill's first unexpected blow failed to kill Mather, the intended victim appealed to Pearce not to allow him to be murdered. The group then agreed to allow Mather half an hour in which to prepare himself for death. They gave him a prayer book and at the end of the appointed time Mather handed the prayer book to Pearce and Greenhill duly dispatched him.

Apart from Pearce and Greenhill, only one man now remained: an Irishman named Matthew Travers who had been sentenced to transportation for life. As the threesome continued on their way, Travers' foot swelled up as a result of a snake bite and he found it increasingly difficult to keep up. When he could go no further, he begged the others to leave him behind. Greenhill and Travers had forged a friendship of sorts and the previously merciless killer now displayed some uncharacteristic reserves of compassion. He and Pearce carried Travers for several days until Greenhill's impatience got the better of him and one afternoon he killed his friend as he slept on the ground.

From then on Pearce and Greenhill watched each other closely. Greenhill jealously guarded the axe and slept with it beneath his head. Fearful that he would go the way of the others, Pearce crept up on the sleeping Greenhill early one morning, wrested the axe from his grasp and killed him with a blow to the head. He dismembered the body and went on his way, taking with him one of Greenhill's arms and part of a leg. Some days later, close to starvation, he happened upon an Aboriginal camp where he found pieces of cooked kangaroo and possum meat around an abandoned campfire. Not long after he emerged into the Derwent Valley where he found a flock of sheep. As he was helping himself to a lamb, a shepherd surprised him with a gun, threatening to shoot him. As luck would have it, the shepherd, an assigned convict, recognised Pearce and gave him shelter for several days.

Now back on the outskirts of civilisation, Pearce soon met up and threw in his lot with a pair of bushrangers, Davis and Churton, who were raiding local sheep stations. For some weeks the trio continued their depredations until, in January 1823, a band of soldiers caught up with them and took them back to Hobart to face justice. Davis and Churton were hanged for their crimes. However, when Pearce, whose crimes were infinitely more heinous, made his long and detailed confession, his story was too fantastically improbable to be believed. As lying was not a hanging offence, he was spared the rope and sent back to Macquarie Harbour.

He did not, however, elude the gallows for much longer. True to form, Pearce again absconded in November 1823 in the company of another convict, Thomas Cox. They headed north, but when they came to a river and Cox admitted he could not swim, Pearce, in a fit of impatient anger, killed him with an axe. The habit of cannibalism must have been deeply ingrained in Pearce because, despite the fact that he still had supplies of food, he cut off and devoured parts of his companion's body.

Perhaps Pearce now knew that the game was up, for he deliberately drew attention to himself by lighting a fire on a beach. Just five days after his escape, Pierce was picked up by a passing ship and taken back to Macquarie Harbour, where the inevitable fate awaited him.

Despite their notoriety, Pearce and his associates were bushrangers only in the sense that they illegally 'ranged' through the countryside. They were a

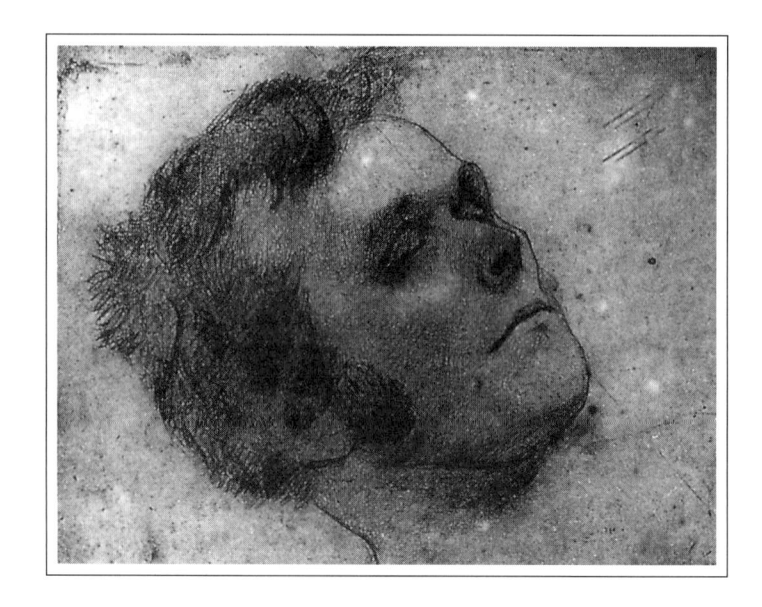

*Alexander Pearce, multiple murderer and self-
confessed cannibal, was the only prisoner to escape
more than once from Macquarie Harbour.*

world away from the popular idea of bushrangers as Australian equivalents of British highwaymen. There was nothing glamorous about their exploits and their demise was accompanied by no expression of public sympathy.

MATTHEW BRADY
A Popular Hero

The first Australian bushranger whose adventures stimulated the popular imagination as much as they frustrated and infuriated the authorities was another escapee from Macquarie Harbour, Matthew Brady. When, on 4 May 1826, Howe, aged 27, died in Hobart at the end of a hangman's rope the event, watched by a large crowd of his supporters and admirers, gave rise to a visible outpouring of public grief. When, at Brady's trial, the judge pronounced the sentence, a number of women in the court wept volubly. In the time between his conviction and his execution, Brady's cell was visited by a constant stream of well-wishers bearing food and flowers, and the lieutenant governor, George Arthur, was besieged with petitions for clemency. In the 22 months since he had been at large, stories of Brady's gallantry towards women and civility towards those whose property he appropriated, as well as his reckless daring, had earned him a cult status that no Australian outlaw had achieved and that only a few would later surpass.

In 1820, Matthew Brady, from Manchester in England and a former soldier in the British Army, was sentenced to death for forgery, a sentence that was commuted to seven years' transportation. On arrival in Sydney Brady was assigned to work for a settler, but he soon proved stubbornly insubordinate and was punished by being assigned to a chain gang. When even this punishment, and a liberal application of the lash, failed to subdue the irrepressible Brady, he was sent to Macquarie Harbour.

Under cover of darkness, one night in June 1824, Brady and 13 other convicts braved the sandbars and other hazards of Hell's Gates in a stolen boat. It was a lucky escape, because they had first tried to seize a boat in which

Matthew Brady

the commandant of the settlement and some of his officers were travelling. Sensing the danger, these officials had rowed themselves out of reach of their would-be assailants, who then availed themselves of an empty whaleboat, which, by a happy coincidence, happened to be moored nearby.

The escaped convicts rowed the whaleboat around the south of the island and landed on the banks of the Derwent in the vicinity of Hobart. They soon provisioned and armed themselves by robbing the house of a settler and so began almost two years of unrestrained defiance of law and authority, during which time Brady and his fellow bandits enjoyed free range of nearly all the settled areas of the island. But during this two year period there were powerful forces working against Brady, forces put into effect by Sir George Arthur which eventually brought him down.

George Arthur, a military disciplinarian

The 39-year-old Arthur arrived in Hobart as lieutenant governor of the convict settlement just three days short of a month before Brady made his dramatic escape from Macquarie Harbour. His appointment, as a replacement for Sorell, marked the beginning of a new regime in Van Diemen's Land. Before accepting the post Arthur, a military man who had seen service in North Africa and the Mediterranean, and who, for eight years, had been commandant of the slave colony British Honduras, had negotiated new powers for himself as lieutenant governor. Unlike his predecessors, he would not have to apply to the governor of New South Wales for permission to grant land or pardons or to extend sentences. He had, indeed, a free hand to run the island very much as he wished, a freedom that was further endorsed the following year when Van Diemen's Land was proclaimed a separate colony with Arthur as its first governor.

Arthur was a military disciplinarian with a bureaucrat's penchant for order. He was, as well, a committed Christian and a zealous moral reformer. His one weakness seemed to be a liking for a glass of port; otherwise he was austere, unsmiling, Calvinist and ascetic. This humourless man was to prove a formidable, and ultimately victorious, adversary for Matthew Brady, the cavalier law-breaker.

Some of the success that Brady's gang enjoyed for so long may well be attributed to Arthur's unpopularity, not only with the convicts, but also with many of the free settlers. One of Arthur's innovations that particularly irked the bulk of the convict population was his institution of the so-called 'field police', a section of the law-enforcement body that consisted of convicts who were still serving their sentences. Those convicts who, through good behaviour and a willingness to collaborate with the authorities, were accorded the privilege of joining this force were despised by their fellows as traitors and resented by free settlers for the authority they enjoyed. To co-operate with such people in their attempts to track down Brady and his cohorts would itself be an act of treachery. Instead, many assigned convicts actively helped the outlaws by giving them food and shelter, and even handing over their masters' weapons. In many cases assigned convicts absconded and joined up with the bushrangers, so that the gang grew steadily larger, at one stage numbering almost 100 members.

Many free settlers, too, felt they had scores to settle with Arthur. The governor's moral crusade was applied to them as much as to the convicts, and those who incurred his displeasure were punished by having the convicts who had been assigned to them, and as a result, their means of

Governor George Arthur

livelihood, removed. A settler who formed a sexual liaison with a convict woman—and such liaisons were not uncommon in a society where women were in short supply—would, if Arthur found out about it, have his labour force taken away. Even fraternising with assigned convicts, or being indulgent or too lenient towards them, could have them reassigned to someone who would treat them with appropriate rigour. In these circumstances, opportunities to help the governor rid himself of the greatest thorn in his side were not infrequently passed up.

A 'gentleman' bushranger

As news of Brady's exploits spread, he acquired a reputation for bravado and style. He became known as a 'gentleman' bushranger, one who offered protection to women and children, and who even extended courtesy and consideration to those of his male victims towards whom he felt no antagonism. On one occasion, Brady returned some stolen property to a surgeon whom he later found had intervened on behalf of a convict who was being brutally flogged.

In one of his most widely reported exploits, Brady and several members of his gang occupied the home of Robert Bethune, a wealthy settler who lived near Hobart. Having satisfied himself that the owner was away, Brady rode up to the house and assembled all the women and servants in one room. He sent the cook into the kitchen to prepare an elaborate meal. When Bethune and a friend returned later in the day, Brady coolly invited them to surrender, which, being unarmed, they readily enough did. Brady then ordered the meal to be served to himself, his gang members and to all the members of the household, while he gallantly played the role of host. The meal over, he relieved his prisoners of their jewellery, watches and other valuables and went on his way.

On another occasion Brady sat on the verandah of a house, chatting with the owner, while members of his gang undertook a room-by-room search for valuables. Brady and prominent members of his gang were also known to frequent, in full view and seemingly without fear of betrayal, inns in Hobart. They also had contacts in Hobart, Launceston and other centres where they could dispose of the proceeds of their robberies. Brady sometimes even went so far as to inform people in advance of his intention to rob and ransack their houses.

Brady's habit of mainly targeting the homes of those seen as oppressors—the likes of magistrates and army officers—was calculated to further enhance the esteem in which he and his gang was held, particularly among the convict classes.

The sheer effrontery of this behaviour was galling to the straightlaced governor, who offered increasingly large rewards for the capture of Brady and his confederates. At first, in August 1824, barely two months after Brady's escape, Arthur offered 10 pounds for the capture of a gang member, increasing the reward to 25 pounds soon afterwards. When these amounts failed to bring in their quarry the price on Brady's head was raised to 300 guineas. A convict who turned in Brady would receive a free pardon and a voyage home. Brady's responded to these offers in a manner calculated to further infuriate the humourless Arthur. With a delicious irony which he doubtless knew would be lost on his adversary, and in a gesture recalling Mike Howe's 'lieutenant governor of the woods' missive to Sorell, Brady made a counter-offer. On the door of a country hotel he pinned up a declaration stating that 'It has caused Matthew Brady much concern that such a person known as Sir George Arthur is still at large', and then going on to offer 20 gallons of rum to whoever could effect his capture. The message ended on a gallant note, designed to enlist the sympathy and admiration of its readers. Brady swore to hang a certain John Priest for his mistreatment of a Mrs Blackwell.

But Arthur could afford to be patient, for he had formidable resources at his command. He had a police force augmented by the inclusion of the convict field force and he had the soldiers of the 40th Regiment who were constantly in the countryside in pursuit, and often close pursuit, of the outlaws. He also had the financial resources to buy co-operation and a native cunning which he used to exploit the finer feelings of his enemy.

One of Brady's proud boasts was that he had never killed anyone in cold blood. But he was responsible, at least indirectly, for several deaths. He was not so sure that he could trust the assigned servants of the households he robbed that he did not take precautions to ensure that they could not inform against him. He would make sure they remembered as little as possible of the circumstances of the robberies by forcing them to drink themselves into a state of stupefaction. Given the rough quality of the whisky and other spirits that were available in the colony, even to affluent households, several of these convicts became violently ill. One, who was unaccustomed to strong liquor, died the next day of his enforced drunkenness.

Brady was responsible, too, indirectly, for the capture and hanging of James McCabe, his second-in-command and a close and trusted associate who was one of his fellow escapees from Macquarie Harbour. McCabe made the mistake of attacking a woman in one of the houses they pillaged. Incensed at this outrage, Brady gave him a beating and threw him out of the gang. In a scuffle between the two men, McCabe was shot in the hand. Left to his own resources, he was soon captured, taken to Hobart and hanged. Efforts by the authorities to elicit from McCabe information about Brady and his whereabouts were unsuccessful.

Nor could Brady always control the actions of the more desperate and violent members of his gang. In one notable incident, two of his men, probably without the knowledge or consent of their leader, called on a man called Renton in the vicinity of Launceston and shot him dead, in retribution, they claimed, for having informed on the movements of the gang.

As the gang grew in size and notoriety, Brady was unable to maintain strict control over its composition and to keep out people he considered undesirable. One particularly unscrupulous and brutal character who was briefly a member of the gang was Mark Jefferies who had, with two companions, escaped from Macquarie Harbour some time after Brady and made his way successfully

Bushrangers such as Matthew Brady were often held in high esteem by a public who enjoyed hearing of their daring exploits.

overland to the settled areas. Jefferies and one of the other escapees survived the journey only by killing and consuming the flesh of the third team member. Jefferies was not long a member of Brady's gang; it seems that he soon quarrelled with Brady and was thrown out. But he was with them long enough to learn about the how the gang operated and where it often hid out. He knew enough when he was captured to inform on the gang's whereabouts and activities, perhaps in the vain hope that some mercy would be shown to him.

But if Jefferies ever had a chance of reprieve, he had forfeited it, along with any begrudging sympathy he might have enjoyed, with one despicable and horrifying crime. Having robbed and murdered a farmer called Tibbs and his stockmen, Jefferies tooks Tibbs' wife and infant prisoner, forcing the woman to carry the baby. When she was unable to keep up with the pace that Jefferies set, her captor, in a fury, snatched the baby and battered it to death.

Captured by Batman

John Batman is remembered mainly for the role he played in the 1830s in the settlement of the Port Phillip district and the eventual establishment of the city of Melbourne. It is less well known that earlier in his career he had settled in Van Diemen's Land and was a noted hunter of bushrangers. Two of his prize catches were the notorious Jefferies, whom he cornered near Launceston and who surrendered without a fight in January 1826, and, just under two months later, a wounded Matthew Brady.

By the time of Jefferies's capture, Brady had developed a strong revulsion for his former colleague. He sent word to Colonel Balfour, who was in charge of the 49th Regiment in Launceston, that he intended to rob the house of a certain Richard Dry and then proceed to Launceston Gaol where Jefferies was being held. He would attack the gaol, release the other prisoners and exact summary justice on the child-murderer. Balfour guessed, correctly, that Brady was not foolhardy enough to storm the gaol, and so dismissed the threat as a piece of empty bravado. But Brady kept at least part of his promise and carried out the scheduled attack on Dry's house. Balfour received news of this outrage while he was dining at the home of a man called Wedge, a well-known hunter of bushrangers. Balfour, Wedge and

John Batman was a successful hunter of bushrangers in Van Diemen's Land.

a party of soldiers set out to do battle with Brady. In the fight that ensued, the bushrangers were driven off, but in a gesture of impertinent daring, they rode into town and attacked and robbed, not the gaol, as Balfour now began to fear, but Wedge's house. The John Priest that Brady had threatened to hang in an addendum to his earlier offer for the capture of the governor was a victim of the skirmish at Dry's house. He was shot in the knee and died a few days later from complications. Ironically, then, Brady had his revenge.

By this time, however, Brady must have known that if he stayed in Van Diemen's Land, his capture was, sooner or later, inevitable. Increasing numbers of men were in pursuit of him and enormous rewards were now being offered by Governor Arthur. In late 1825 he and members of his gang attempted to flee the island in a stolen boat, but the attempt was abandoned when the boat was sighted. A later attempt to leave the island in another stolen boat was foiled by rough weather.

A combination of Arthur's cunning, the treachery of a convict collaborator and compassion, linked perhaps to a surprising gullibility on Brady's part, eventually led to the elusive bushranger's downfall. A convict named Cowan was sent into the bush wearing broken leg irons. He met up with some of Brady's men who, assuming he was an escapee from a road gang, welcomed him into their gang. He stayed with the gang for some time, taking part in their raids and ingratiating himself with them. But he was merely waiting for the right moment. When the opportunity came, he made his escape and reported the gang's whereabouts to a Lieutenant Williams of the 40th Regiment. Williams' men surprised the outlaws, capturing a number of them and sending others fleeing in different directions. In the exchange of fire, Brady was wounded in the thigh, although he escaped with the help of two of his comrades.

He remained at large for only a few days longer. John Batman, with the help of Aboriginal trackers, ran him to ground near the North Esk River in the north of the island and the wounded Brady had no choice but to surrender.

The ensuing trial and its aftermath were, of course, foregone conclusions. When Brady mounted the scaffold after receiving communion from a priest, four other felons accompanied him. One of them was James Bryant, one of the 13 who had escaped with Brady from Macquarie Harbour and who had stayed with him all the time they were at large; another was Mark Jefferies. To die beside Jefferies was for Brady a hideous indignity and one which, perhaps, was consciously devised by Arthur as a final insult for his hated adversary.

The death of Matthew Brady did not spell the end of bushranging in Van Diemen's Land, but it did, for the time at least, remove the threat of marauding gangs that terrorised settlers on a large scale. With the removal of Brady, settlers could move with relative confidence into hitherto unoccupied areas.

MARTIN CASH
From Outlaw to Landowner

The last significant Vandemonian bushranger, Martin Cash, was, like Matthew Brady, a man of charismatic charm whose exploits aroused a good deal of public admiration. Also like Brady, he began his career as a bushranger by escaping from a place of secondary punishment. But unlike Brady, and almost all other bushrangers, he did not die violently or in ignominy. Despite his tempestuous early career as a lawbreaker and repeated absconder from custody, and despite being convicted of murder and sentenced to death, Cash died a respected landholder on his farm near Hobart in 1877 at the relatively ripe old age of 67.

Cash took to bushranging after escaping, not from Macquarie Harbour, but from the equally grim prison that replaced it in 1833 on an isolated peninsula about 100 kilometres south of Hobart. After almost ten years, Macquarie Harbour was proving too remote for convenience and too difficult to maintain. Arthur therefore decided to establish a new penal colony closer to the centre of administration. It was named in his honour and, perhaps appropriately for a man of such punitive moral instincts, it is what he is now best remembered for.

Cash arrived at Port Arthur in 1840 at the age of 30 by a rather circuitous route. By the time he got there he had already served out the seven-year sentence which had seen him transported to Sydney from his native Ireland in 1827 at the tender age of 17. It is not absolutely clear for what offence the young Cash was convicted. According to his autobiography, which Cash supposedly dictated to a fellow former convict and which was first published in 1870, he shot and wounded a fellow youth whom he found embracing his girlfriend. Here, as elsewhere, Cash may have been embellishing the truth in the interests of enhancing his image. Other sources suggest that he was involved in nothing more romantic than a common case of housebreaking and theft.

Given his turbulent later career, Cash was surprisingly compliant during his early years in the colony. He was assigned to a squatter in the Hunter Valley, north-west of Sydney, gave no trouble and did not try to abscond. His exemplary behaviour may be attributable to the fact that he formed an attachment to the young wife of a storekeeper who lived nearby. Eliza Clifford, known as Bessie, was about 22 years old when Cash first met her, and, as he put it, 'appeared to be at the time the most beautiful person I had ever beheld'. She had married her husband in Britain while he was still an army officer. He seems to have been a rather dissolute character who, soon after his marriage, sold his army commission, spent his money recklessly and, using money provided by wealthy relatives, sailed with his wife to New South Wales to make a new start. The change of scene, however, did not bring about a change in habits and, by the time Bessie and Martin Cash met and were strongly attracted to each other,

Driven by a guard wielding a fearsome whip, a team of convicts laboriously hauls a plough on the farm at the Port Arthur prison settlement.

the young woman was disenchanted with the marriage. When Clifford, tired of his present situation, announced his intention of moving from the district, Bessie decided to throw in her lot with Cash who, fortuitously, had just obtained his ticket-of-leave.

The move to Van Diemen's Land

For the next couple of years, Cash found work in New South Wales on the cattle and sheep stations that were being established as settlement spread west of the Great Dividing Range. He was forced to flee from the colony, however, when he was observed branding stolen cattle, an offence that could earn him transportation to the dreaded penal colony at Norfolk Island. Cash, it seems, was innocent of any criminal intent: he was branding the cattle for a friend whom he thought had come by them honestly. But, given his convict past, he was unlikely to be believed and he and Bessie escaped to Hobart, where they arrived in 1837.

Finding no work in Hobart, Cash and Bessie went north where, at a place near Launceston, Cash was given work, along with accommodation, as a harvester. He was forced to leave again soon afterwards when, having been wrongly accused and subsequently acquitted of stealing a watch, he assaulted the arresting police. He next took up a job as manager of a dairy farm near Campbell Town, south of Launceston. While Cash was absent from the farm, some poultry was stolen. The stolen property was discovered in the possession of a man whom he had allowed to stay on the farm. However, Cash was arrested and convicted of the theft. As a former convict, and with his recent violence against police also counting against him, he received little sympathy and was sentenced to a further term of seven years. So began his decline into a second life of crime.

Hardly had Cash begun work on a road-building project near Hobart than he seized an opportunity to make off into the bush and hide there until he could sneak off under cover of darkness. He was soon recaptured, however, betrayed by the light of his campfire. He was taken to Oatlands, about 60 kilometres north of Hobart, where he was sentenced to an extra 18 months, the first nine of them to be spent working in a chain gang. He spent two weeks in the Oatlands gaol, and was then assigned to a gang at a place called Jerusalem. He immediately began planning his escape.

On the advice of another convict to whom he confided his intentions, he feigned illness, supposing that a visit to the doctor would present an opportunity to abscond. Instead, the suspicious overseer hauled him in front of a magistrate on a charge of malingering and Cash was given three days' solitary confinement in a cell. At the end of this sentence, while he was being held in a yard waiting to be returned to his chain gang, he managed to get hold of a large stone and break apart the chain that connected his leg irons. He then scaled the palisade fence that surrounded the compound and once again concealed himself in the bush.

It was about three o'clock on a winter afternoon when Cash made his escape. About eight hours later he broke into a house and stole provisions for his journey, which was in the direction of Campbell Town and Bessie. Travelling by night, and lying low by day, Cash spent the long, idle hours patiently hammering away with stones at his leg irons until he was free of them.

While Cash was in the Oatlands gaol awaiting assignment to a chain gang, he had made friends with a prisoner who talked of a house in the vicinity of Campbell Town where he had previously been an assigned convict. He gave Cash a detailed description of the location, layout and contents of the house and even told him of a window which would provide easy access. Cash managed to find the house, entered through the window as instructed and helped himself to a complete change of clothes, as well as a few spare garments and a supply of food. Now attired in the garb of respectability, Cash could more safely venture into Campbell Town and seek out Bessie. He entered under cover of darkness, waited near a house which he knew she often visited and soon met up with her in the street. They hastily made plans for their escape together and arranged a rendezvous for later in the evening.

The local schoolmaster, however, lurking behind a fence, overheard their plans and when Bessie had gone he accosted Cash with a shotgun. The two men struggled and Cash was slightly wounded as the gun discharged. He managed to escape, knocking his adversary to the ground and narrowly avoiding the police who, alerted by the disturbance, soon arrived on the scene.

Thanks either to the incompetence of the local police, or her own cunning, Bessie was able to sneak out later that night and find Cash, and arrange to meet him again early the next morning. This she did, bringing provisions with her and a penknife with which she cleaned Cash's gunshot wound. They made a further assignation for that evening at the house of a sympathetic acquaintance outside the town. That night, armed with two bundles of clothes and other provisions, the pair struck southwards, bound for Hobart. Three times on the way the venture came close to catastrophe. On one occasion a convict shepherd recognised Cash and bailed him up at gunpoint, only to be disarmed and left tied to a tree by his wily adversary. At another time Cash was preparing to enter and rob a farmhouse when he was unexpectedly set upon and felled by a blow to the head, but again he contrived to escape. On yet another occasion both Cash and Bessie were captured by settlers and brought before a magistrate on suspicion of being up to no good in the bush. As they were not recognised and no wrongdoing could be proved against them they were let go free.

Bad weather forced them to stay six weeks in Hobart, during which time they remained undetected. They then headed south to the Huon River region, where Cash found regular work with a boatbuilder. He and Bessie lived happily here for about a year, saving money for a berth to Melbourne where they would finally be out of reach of the authorities. Even here, however, the precariousness of their situation was brought home to them when they were recognised by a stranger who addressed them both by their names, but who assured them he had no reason for or intention of informing on them. He proved as good as his word.

When Cash's term of employment came to an end, he and Bessie returned to Hobart where they took up temporary lodgings. Cash was recognised at a baker's shop by a woman who had been a neighbour in Campbell Town. Concerned that he might be betrayed, Cash immediately found new lodgings on the outskirts of the city, but when he returned to collect his belongings, he was seized by six constables and taken into custody.

Three weeks later he was brought before magistrate John Price, whose gloating sarcasm in sentencing him to an extra four years, which were to be served 'at hard labour' at Port Arthur, must have riled the young Irishman. 'I intend,' said Price, 'to place you where you will be safe for some time to come, and thereby save you the trouble and expense of peregrinating through the country.' He further promised Cash that if this did not bring about the desired reformation, 'I shall see what else can be done for you'.

An almost successful escape attempt

Nature could hardly have provided a more perfect site for a prison than the Tasman Peninsula, where Port Arthur was established. Escape from it was made extremely difficult, if not virtually impossible, both by its isolation and by the fact that to reach the island's 'mainland' one had to cross two very narrow isthmuses or 'necks' of land. The first of these, ominously named Eaglehawk Neck, led to an intermediate peninsula, the Forestier Peninsula, which in turn narrowed to another land bridge, known in the 19th century as East Bay Neck. Escape by land, then, would entail passing undetected through both narrow necks. Eaglehawk Neck was guarded not only by human sentries but by a phalanx of half-starved guard dogs, each chained to a post and each just out of reach of the dog on either side of it. Any escapee trying to run this grisly gauntlet would be likely to be torn to pieces and could hardly hope to escape detection.

Cash was determined to escape even before he arrived at Port Arthur, but he bided his time, waiting for the onset of warmer weather and for an opportunity to survey the lie of the land. A failed escape attempt by six prisoners soon after his arrival, for which each of them received 100 lashes, may also have had a cautionary influence on him. They failed at least partly because they had no understanding of the local topography.

His chance to assess the dangers of escaping and the odds against succeeding came one day when he was sent to Mount Arthur, a high hill a little way outside the penal colony, to take supplies to some troops that were stationed there. From this vantage point he could see the line of dogs across Eaglehawk Neck and the sentries that were scattered through other parts of the peninsula.

Not long afterwards, while working on a site near the water, Cash was verbally abused by the overseer of his gang. Stung by this unexpected attack, Cash seized the man and hurled him into the water and, while the other convicts and soldiers were occupied with fishing him out, he made his bolt for freedom. He made it overland to a point on Norfolk Bay near Eaglehawk Neck and then plunged into the reputedly shark-infested waters and reached the shores of the Forestier Peninsula, thus bypassing Eaglehawk Neck and its line of savage dogs. He again struck out overland in what he thought was the direction of East Bay Neck, but lost his way and had to retrace his steps. As he stumbled across the peninsula a second time, ravaged by hunger and on the point of collapse—he had been at liberty almost five days and had had no food—he was recaptured by a search party.

On being taken before the commandant, a man called O'Hara Booth who was noted for his extreme severity, Cash feigned contriteness and, to his surprise, was spared the almost inevitable flogging. As well as saving him from the agony of such a brutal punishment, the reprieve also kept alive the hope of a later escape. Escapees who were flogged were then forced to work in irons with a heavy wooden block attached to them. As it was, Cash's adventure earned him a sentence of 18 months hard labour in chains.

Kavanagh and Jones

Cash's bold bid for freedom had won him the admiration of his fellow convicts and even the respect of some of the soldiers. He was soon sought out by two fellow convicts, Kavanagh and Jones, who themselves had plans to escape and who thought that Cash's knowledge of the local geography and the experience gained on his previous attempt could be of use to them. Kavanagh and Jones had been transported to Port Arthur for bushranging in New South Wales, and Jones claimed to have heard favourable reports of Cash when he was in the Hunter Valley region. Cash at this time was employed in collecting stone from a quarry in which the two former bushrangers were working, a circumstance that gave the three men ample opportunity to work out the details of a plan.

Kavanagh had access to provisions from a compliant official and had hidden a bundle of them close to the quarry. The escape was set for 26 December 1842 and at the appointed time the three men scrambled up the sides of the quarry and headed for the nearby scrub. The guards, taken by surprise, and with their senses perhaps dulled in the aftermath of Christmas celebrations, failed to apprehend them and the escapees were soon deep in the bush and safe from immediate danger.

The men, led by Cash, made their way to a point below Eaglehawk Neck, where they lay concealed for two days before attempting the swim across to the Forestier Peninsula. When they felt the coast was clear, they stripped off their clothes, securing them to their bodies with belts, and scrambled into the water. The swim was made difficult by buffeting waves and when the three struggled ashore they found that their clothes had been swept away.

The naked men spent a night sheltering as best they could in the prickly scrub. The next morning they were fortunate to come upon a hut which accommodated a convict gang that was working in the area. As the gang was already at work, the escapees were able to overcome the sole overseer who was left in charge, tying him to a post as they helped themselves to clothes, boots and food.

Guessing that the guard at East Bay Neck would be reinforced following their escape, Cash and his two companions remained hidden in the bush for two more days, at one stage narrowly missing detection by a search party that passed within several metres of them. Cash argued that their best chance of escaping the Forestier Peninsula was to swim across a part of the bay known as the 'Narrows', a little to the west of East Bay Neck. Jones and Kavanagh, though, opted to face the hazards of East Bay Neck rather than to risk drowning in the strong currents of the bay, and Cash deferred to them. Under cover of darkness they made for the Neck, sometimes crawling through the undergrowth, sometimes retreating as they came close to sentry boxes, and at one stage attracting the unwanted attentions of a small farm dog. Eventually, coming close to a sentry box and observing two guards saunter off towards the water's edge, they sprinted forwards, scaled a fence and were soon clear of the peninsula.

A gang of three

Cash, Jones and Kavanagh now made eastwards towards the settled areas around Hobart. They helped themselves to some provisions from an isolated hut occupied by a family, warning their bewildered victims not to raise the alarm. Near the town of Sorell they stormed into a prosperous-looking farmhouse, pretending to be armed, and left bearing a gun with ammunition, new clothes and a generous supply of food. Cash helped himself to a top hat which he later sometimes wore for effect in carrying out robberies. They decided that their only option was to take to bushranging, in which Kavanagh and Jones were already experienced, even taking into account that it would almost inevitably lead them to the gallows. According to Cash's later account, they made a pact that they would not resort to 'ruffianism', would fight only to protect themselves and would not inflict unnecessary harm on victims of their predations. By and large, during the 20 months they remained at large they adhered to the standards they set themselves.

Convict bolters in Van Diemen's Land attacked settlers' huts in remote areas, stealing food and ammunition and making off with sheep and horses.

With only one gun in their possession, however, they were hardly in a position to pursue their newly adopted vocation. Large properties employed shepherds who lived in outlying huts and had guns and ammunition for the protection of their charges. A shepherd's hut near a place called Prosser's Plain was, therefore, the gang's next target. This yielded a single-barrelled gun along with some powder and shot, willingly yielded to them by a frightened woman whom they found alone in the hut. They found another willing accomplice at their next calling place, where, as luck would have it, they were met and welcomed by the wife of a Port Arthur convict who was known to Jones and Kavanagh. With the aid of the woman, they picked up a double-barrelled shotgun, more powder and shot, and a swag of other provisions.

At the next place they raided, an inn at Bagdad, about halfway between Hobart and Oatlands, they learned a lesson that was to stand them and later bushrangers in good stead, the neglect of which would eventually bring the last of the great Australian bushrangers to his doom. The lesson was simply that, while conducting a raid, you do not allow anyone to escape and alert the authorities. A member of the household whom Jones was guarding contrived to give him the slip, causing the bushrangers to make an early departure and depriving them of further spoils. They did, however, carry off a quantity of clothes which meant that henceforth they did not need to appear publicly in remnants of prison clothing.

The raid on the Woolpack Inn

Despite their pact not to resort to unnecessary aggression, Cash and Co, as they came to be known, were prepared to be provocative and seemed keen to make an early and dramatic impression on the colony. Having embarked on a life of outlawry, they were, it seems, ready to test their mettle and confront the forces of law and order head on. They set their sights on the Woolpack Inn near New Norfolk, where they knew from information given to them by a shepherd that a party of soldiers was stationed. Indeed, as they had no reason to be confident that the shepherd would be discreet, they strongly suspected that their intended raid was now common knowledge.

Sure enough, when they arrived after dark one evening and had bailed up the landlady and her two adult sons and three men who were drinking at the bar—the landlord, a Mr Stoddart, was not there at the time—they noticed a group of men emerge from a hut in the grounds of the inn and move stealthily towards the building. Cash stationed himself near the door and fired at the leader of the advancing party, severely wounding him in the chest. The assault on the would-be law enforcers had the desired effect and the rest of the advancing group beat a strategic retreat, disappearing into the darkness.

Unknown to Cash, his two companions had also made a less than heroic exit, for when, after satisfying himself that the soldiers had in fact left the scene, he returned to the bar to find his victims still cowering in corners, there was no sign of Jones and Kavanagh. Seizing a cask of brandy—the only booty from this raid—Cash went out into the night where he soon discovered his cohorts concealed in some bushes. Thinking that their leader had been killed in the exchange of fire and that a similar fate for them was imminent, they had made good their escape. They later learnt from a shepherd that two of the soldiers had been wounded, although one of them only lightly, and that the inhabitants of the inn had supposed that Jones and Kavanagh had been killed in the crossfire. To prevent this shepherd from alerting authorities of their immediate whereabouts, the three bandits plied him liberally with the stolen liquor.

With their new career now so publicly launched—the affair was prominently, though very inaccurately, reported in the Hobart press—it was imperative that they find a secure hideout. They made for a small farmhouse that belonged to a family called Bean with whom Cash was acquainted. Here they were cordially received and, given the poverty of the inhabitants, generously entertained. This dwelling was situated near the foot of a hillock, known as Mount Dromedary, whose rocky overhangs and elevated situation seemed to offer the trio both adequate shelter and a vantage point over the surrounding countryside. Mount Dromedary, then, became their headquarters. On the top of this hill they even contrived to erect a kind of crude fortress of logs and branches which would afford them some rudimentary protection in case of attack.

Bessie visits the fortress

Bean was able through an intermediary to get a message to Bessie Clifford, who was in domestic service in Hobart, informing her of Cash's whereabouts and suggesting that she join the gang. Aware that she was under surveillance and conscious that she was being trailed, she nevertheless managed to elude her followers by unexpectedly flagging down a coach bound for Launceston and, having left behind her unwanted attendants, alighting soon afterwards and proceeding undetected towards the appointed meeting place.

Having Bessie, or 'Mrs Cash' as he referred to her, at the Dromedary hideout obviously filled an emotional need for Cash—and, at this stage at least, for Bessie too—but it was a risky undertaking and one that sowed the seeds of Cash's eventual downfall. In all his raids on properties, Cash was meticulously solicitous of the welfare of the women and children he encountered, never failing to reassure them that they would come to no harm. He was, accordingly, all the more concerned for the safety of his beloved Bessie and soon realised that in their situation he could not guarantee her even the degree of protection that he could extend to his victims.

The precariousness of her situation became even more pronounced after the gang attacked the wealthy Shone household not far from New Norfolk. As well as a rich haul of jewellery and money, Cash also helped himself to dresses and other items of female apparel as a gift for Bessie. As a result of this bold robbery, in which not only the Shone family but a number of guests were relieved on their possessions, the searches for the offenders were intensified in the area. From his hideout Cash could see the search parties combing the countryside and, becoming nervous about Bessie's situation, decided that she should leave them and go back to Hobart.

She was accordingly escorted part of the way and then left to find her way into town, where she again came under surveillance. She was arrested and jailed soon afterwards when she tried to sell off some of the fine clothing that been stolen from the Shones.

An ultimatum

Bessie's arrest and imprisonment prompted a response from Cash reminiscent of Matthew Brady's peremptory letter to George Arthur. Raiding a wealthy household at Dunrobin, near Hamilton, the gang had the owner, Charles Kerr, take down a letter to the governor of Van Diemen's Land, Sir John Franklin, threatening to 'flog' him personally and 'wreak vengeance' on other prominent people in the colony if 'Mrs Cash' was not 'released forthwith'. Another letter in a similar vein was sent to the Shone household whom Cash, rather illogically, held responsible for Bessie's imprisonment.

This was still early in 1843 and for the next few months the Cash gang raided a number of wealthy landholders and lived comfortably enough off their takings, frequently enjoying the company and hospitality of the Beans. As it turned out Bessie did not remain long in custody but was released, probably not as a result of the letters but more likely as a temptation to lure Cash into Hobart to seek her out.

Cash's initial pleasure on hearing this news was dashed when he learnt through a friend that Bessie had taken up residence with Thomas Pratt, a Hobart tradesman. The injury was deepened by the realisation that this liaison was not a new one and that it probably predated Bessie's visit to the Mount Dromedary hideout.

A mission of revenge

As time went on and periods of inaction gave Cash time to brood about his betrayal, his anger against Bessie intensified. His jealousy was fuelled even more, perhaps, by his perception of a growing intimacy between Jones and the woman of the household where they so often found shelter. Eventually, in August 1843, Cash's patience and good judgment gave way. He and Kavanagh went into Hobart with the intention of finding and shooting Bessie and her 'paramour'. Arriving undetected in the town, they went to the house of a friendly Irishman whom they had met at the Beans' house. He agreed to accompany them to help find where Bessie and Pratt were living, which was rumoured to be in the vicinity of the Bells of Scotland Inn in Murray Street. As they approached this inn, the Irishman casually enquired of a passer-by if he knew the whereabouts of the pair. By a stroke of misfortune, this man happened to be a constable who, his suspicions aroused, looked around and, recognising Cash standing nearby, alerted his companion that 'this is the party we want'. The constable and his companion immediately gave chase. Cash's Irish friend made off in the ensuing melee, but Cash was pursued, not only by the two constables but also by a number of citizens who quickly joined in.

Cash was a formidable runner and quickly put distance between himself and his pursuers but he lost his advantage when he ran into a cul-de-sac and had to retrace his steps. Unable to force his way past a large man who barred his way, Cash drew one of his two pistols and fired, mortally wounding his adversary. As

Martin Cash, photographed long after his bushranging days had ended.

others converged on the scene, Cash was forced to the ground and captured. Almost simultaneously Kavanagh was wounded in another scuffle and surrendered to a magistrate.

The next morning Cash was visited by the same John Price who had previously sentenced him to his term at Port Arthur and who now informed him that the man he had shot, a constable named Winstanley, had died of his wounds and that he would therefore go on trial for murder. Cash and Kavanagh were tried together and both, predictably, were sentenced to hang. But even in his reduced and wretched circumstances, Cash must have retained something of his old charisma. As he awaited execution, he was called upon by a succession of sympathetic visitors, including soldiers and other officials who had been his staunch adversaries. Some of these, perhaps, interceded on his behalf with the governor. The day before the scheduled hanging the prison chaplain informed him that he had been granted a reprieve of ten days on the grounds that the chaplain did not consider him yet ready to meet his death, and just over a week later the chaplain brought him the news that his, and Kavanagh's, sentences had been commuted to life imprisonment, subject to royal approval.

It took about 15 months for this approval to arrive, during which time Cash was held in the Hobart gaol, still officially under sentence of death. About seven months after his trial, Cash was reunited briefly with Jones who, after Cash's and Kavanagh's arrest, had joined up with two recent escapees from a road gang and had continued raiding properties, operating from Mount Dromedary and using the Beans' hut as shelter and as a place to store their stolen booty. Less discreet than when Cash was in charge, Jones' gang was traced to the Beans' hut, which was surrounded and set fire to. One of Jones' partners was shot and killed, the other was captured, and Jones, almost blinded by a blast of buckshot that hit him in the face, was taken into custody. The Beans, too, were arrested but were later released.

Jones' fate was quickly sealed, possibly because in one of his robberies he had tortured a woman to force her to reveal where the household money was hidden. He was sentenced to death and, despite the terrible injury he had received, was quickly executed.

Norfolk Island

When Queen Victoria's official approval was received, Cash was removed from Hobart and sent to the convict colony on Norfolk Island, where he was again united with Kavanagh. But like his reunion with Jones, this one was destined to be relatively brief. Within a year of Cash's arrival, Kavanagh took part in a murderous mutiny against the authorities. For his part in this uprising he, along with 12 others, was hanged in October 1846. Cash was now in his mid-thirties and his taste for such reckless adventure, especially when it was so clearly doomed to failure, had perhaps now subsided. He was among the minority of prisoners who took no part in the revolt.

On Norfolk Island Cash weathered and even thrived under the tyrannical regime of his old nemesis John Price, who arrived on Norfolk Island as commandant just after the mutiny and who oversaw the trials and executions. By 1853, when he was granted a ticket-of-leave, Cash had married Mary Bennett, the widow of a convict, and was a trusted prisoner. He had even been appointed as one of several convict 'constables'.

After his release, Cash spent some time working in the Hobart Botanic Gardens, then, after a spell in New Zealand, he returned to Tasmania and purchased a farm at Glenorchy, near Hobart, where he spent the rest of his days.

EARLY MAINLAND BUSHRANGERS
Wild Colonial Boys

When Lachlan Macquarie was governor of New South Wales, his main concerns with bushranging were with the recurrent outbreaks in Van Diemen's Land. Similar 'epidemics' of bushranging on the mainland did not occur until the 1820s—Macquarie left the colony in 1821—and coincided, probably not by chance, with a determined and officially promoted toughening of attitudes to convict discipline and the removal of many of the privileges that serving convicts had enjoyed under Macquarie.

By the standards of his time, Macquarie was a humane administrator whose approach to the penal system was rehabilitative rather than primarily punitive. While he had no aversion to the rope and the lash as means of maintaining discipline and suppressing outlawry, and while he supported lieutenant governors Davey and Sorell in their ruthless suppression of the Vandemonian bushrangers, he was generous in rewarding good behaviour with early remission of sentences and insisting that convicts be treated fairly.

Macquarie was anxious to see the colony develop into a civil society rather than a festering prison, and he encouraged emancipists to build careers and prosper in the colony by appointing them to positions of trust and responsibility and by granting them land. Not surprisingly these policies, while applauded by many, were vigorously opposed by some people of influence and power—among them John Macarthur and the Reverend Samuel Marsden—who made their dissatisfaction known to the authorities in England.

In 1820 the British government sent Judge and King's Commissioner John

Thomas Bigge to New South Wales to report on the state of the colony. In his report Bigge found fault with many aspects of Macquarie's administration and was severely critical of what he saw as his leniency towards convicts and his attitude towards emancipists. Wounded by Bigge's report, an ailing and ageing Macquarie—he was now 60—left the colony and was replaced by Thomas Brisbane, who was given the task of implementing Bigge's recommendations. Brisbane went some way towards doing this, but it was his successor, Ralph Darling, who took over as governor in 1825, who instituted a regime of draconian severity.

Governor Sir Ralph Darling, disliked by settlers and convicts alike

Darling's punitive instincts are perhaps best exemplified in the famous case of two soldiers, Sudds and Thompson, who were convicted of stealing and sentenced to seven years' transportation. Darling arbitrarily increased the severity of the sentence by decreeing that the two men would serve out their time in chain gangs and that they would work in leg irons and iron collars attached by chains to the leg irons. One of them, Sudds, died while working under these conditions. The chain gang is a potent symbol of Ralph Darling's period of office. In his time chain gangs moved inexorably further out from the centre of settlement, opening up and building roads to the west and the north. The remoteness of their situation and the harsh conditions under which they worked gave convicts both the opportunity and the motivation to abscond.

Many did abscond during the 1820s and 1830s. Their depredations made life difficult and often dangerous for settlers in the more remote districts north to the Hunter Valley and west to Bathurst. Most of these bushrangers achieved little celebrity; many were little more than petty thieves who survived, singly or in small gangs, by pilfering from farms and homesteads. In 1822 more than 30 so-called bushrangers were hanged in Sydney, many of them for a single offence of stealing from a farm. Others, however, gained temporary notoriety as perpetrators of violence. A few were widely admired for their deeds of daring and their defiance of authority. Governor Darling's deep unpopularity, among convicts and free settlers alike, no doubt helped boost the appeal of those who successfully flouted his authority.

Jack Donohue

One lawbreaker whom the populace really took to its heart was a small, fleet-footed, quick-tempered, blond, blue-eyed Irish youth known as Jack Donohue. Donohue and a changing group of accomplices ranged around the Nepean Valley to the west and south-west of Sydney, even moving as far west as the Bathurst region, for almost three years in the late 1820s. Donohue's fame was so great that his exploits, real and imagined, and with appropriately exaggerated heroics, were related in a number of popular ballads. These were sung and recited with gusto in Sydney hostelries until Governor Darling, seeing himself gratuitously insulted by such revelry, banned the practice and threatened to close down any hotel that allowed it. Donohue became known as the first of the 'wild colonial boys' and the famed ballad of that name owes its inspiration to him.

Donohue arrived in Sydney as a convict in January 1825 at the tender age of 19, already with a history of political activism in the cause of Irish nationalism. His sentence was transportation for life for a crime vaguely designated as 'intent to commit felony'. His anti-establishment credentials in his native land soon manifested themselves in his new environment. He was assigned to a farmer in the Parramatta area, but his insubordinate nature soon got him into trouble and he was sentenced to work in chains in a road gang. He was next assigned to an army surgeon and was given the job of supervising a pig farm near Quakers Hill. The young Irishman took advantage of the relative freedom of movement that this situation permitted and in December 1827, in company with two other assigned convicts, he absconded. The three escapees managed to acquire arms and held up the bullock wagons that slowly moved along the Windsor Road, laden with farm produce. Their success was short-lived, however, and in March 1828 Donohue and his companions, George Kilroy and Bill Smith, were arrested and sentenced to death. Had the scheduled sentence been carried out, Donohue would have become yet another anonymous statistic in the story of Australian bushranging instead of one of its star players.

Map showing Hawkesbury River, Richmond, Windsor, Windsor Road, Penrith, Blacktown, Parramatta, Liverpool, Jack Donohoe shot here, Campbelltown.

As the condemned men were being moved from the court to the police cells in Sydney, Donohue made a dash for freedom, managing to elude his pursuers. His companions were duly hanged, but Donohue remained at large with a price on his head. He made for the west, and in company with other escapees began raids on the newly established settlements in the region around Bathurst. Gradually they moved further afield until their operations covered almost all the settled outlying areas of the colony. They had little trouble in profitably disposing of unwanted stolen goods; there was no shortage of settlers willing to trade these for money or for other commodities of use to the bushrangers.

Donohue's career was again almost brought to a premature end in late 1828 when a troupe of police surprised and shot two members of the gang as they sat around a campfire not far from Bathurst. When the other gang members returned from a raid the police opened fire, killing or wounding a number and then, over the next few days, tracking down the remainder until only one—Donohue himself—remained mysteriously at large.

At various times, Donohue was associated with different accomplices. For some time after his narrow escape near Bathurst he teamed up with another Irish bushranger, Will Underwood, who operated mainly in the Nepean area. More commonly he worked with Jack Walmesley, an escapee from a chain gang, and Bill Webber. It was in company with Underwood that Donohue held up one of his most famous victims, the 'flogging parson', the Reverend Samuel Marsden, and relieved him of the sum of four pounds, an exploit that would have helped endear the outlaw to a large section of the population.

Rumours about Donohue abounded in the colony. Stories about 'Bold Jack', as he was commonly referred to, seemed to be on everyone's lips. At one stage he was rumoured to have been killed by Aboriginal people, at another to have fled to New Zealand. There is a story that he once bailed up the explorer Charles Sturt but, on recognising his victim, gallantly let him pass unmolested. Gallantry was a quality often attributed to him, as was a habit of carrying out his robberies immaculately dressed and wearing a top hat. WC Wentworth's newspaper, the *Australian*, once reported that he had recently been seen on the streets of Sydney, nonchalantly drinking ginger beer. Indeed the press, and particularly the *Australian*, while not openly supporting Donohue did much to mythologise him by regularly reporting on his exploits. Wentworth was a bitter opponent of Darling and a strong supporter of Macquarie's emancipist policies, and he was ever willing to publish news, or even rumours, that would add to the governor's discomfiture.

By 1830 the price on Donohue's head had increased tenfold, from 20 to 200 pounds and, in the same year, Darling introduced his notorious Bushranging Act which, in extending the terms of an 1825 Act, allowed the arbitrary arrest of anyone suspected of being an absconder and gave police greatly increased powers of search and entry. It also decreed draconian sentences for those engaged in or assisting bushrangers and other offenders.

But by now the end was near for Donohue. Early in September 1830 a troupe of police spotted Donohue, Walmesley and Webber from a distance near Bringelly in the Campbelltown area. The police managed to get within close range before their presence was detected. The bushrangers took refuge behind trees, but one of the police managed to get Donohue in his sights and killed him with a shot through the head.

The popular ballad that purported to tell the story of 'Bold Jack Donohue', reported that:

> ... as he closed his mournful eyes, he bade the world adieu, Crying, 'Convicts all, pray for the soul of bold Jack Donohue!'

In fact, the truth was more prosaic. The bullet that struck him down brought to an end, not only Donohue's life, but also the string of obscenities with which he was taunting his pursuers.

Webber and Walmesley escaped as darkness fell. Webber was cornered and shot dead about a month later and soon after that Walmesley was captured. He was sentenced to death but was reprieved when he agreed to inform on the many free settlers who had sheltered or collaborated with the Donohue gang.

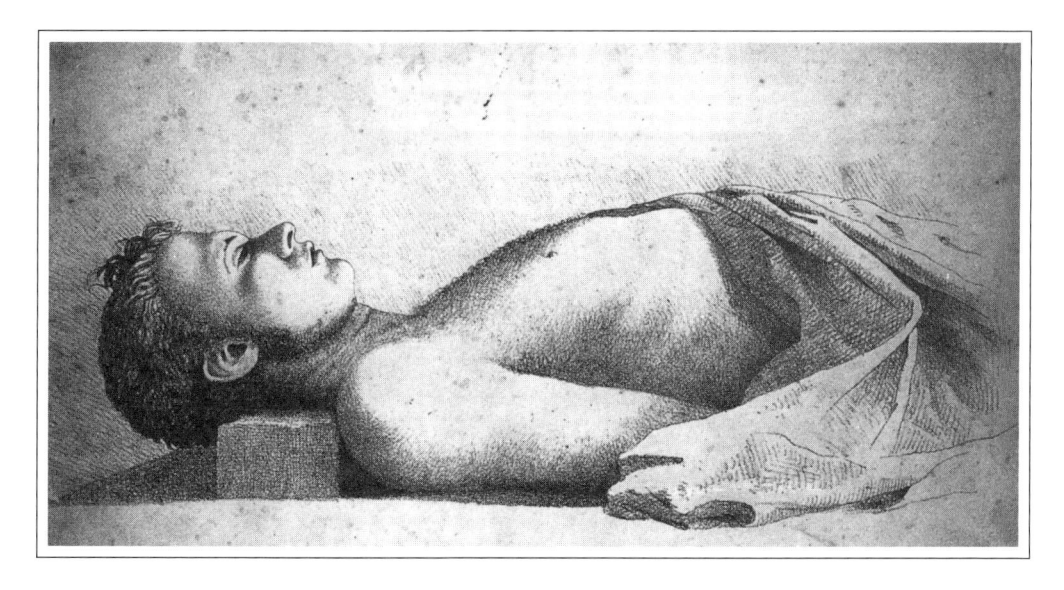

Jack Donohue, sketched after his death

John Lynch, a multiple axe-murderer

In stark contrast to Donohue, Brady and other bushrangers who aroused a degree of public sympathy, was another Irishman, John Lynch. At the end of his life Lynch inspired nothing short of universal revulsion. His hanging at Berrima gaol in April 1842 brought to an end a murderous spree that had brought about the deaths of at least ten people, including those of a 16-year-old boy and a 14-year-old girl. At his trial Lynch was coolly unrepentant about the carnage he had perpetrated; indeed he seemed to have taken pride in his outrages, believing himself, so he claimed, to have been directed by divine inspiration.

Lynch was a short, fair-complexioned, brown-haired young man with an insidiously engaging manner. He had the uncanny ability to gain the confidence of strangers and to engage their sympathy for his supposed mishaps and misfortunes. He was a most plausible and quick-witted liar who often displayed a gift for imaginative invention. He was also greatly adept at covering his tracks. He was, in fact, hanged for only one murder—the last he committed. Until this one was discovered, Lynch had for several months been living on and administering a farm after murdering the owner and his family and successfully explaining away their sudden disappearance. Lynch's earlier murders, committed over a period of several years, had remained undetected and came to light only after he was arrested and his history investigated. The facts about how many of these killings occurred may never have become known had Lynch not, the day before his execution, made a long and detailed confession to the prison chaplain and the attendant magistrate.

The trial in which Lynch was convicted was not his first trial, nor was it the first time he had been accused of murder. In 1835 he had been tried for stealing a saddle from the farm to which he had been assigned but had been acquitted. Soon after this acquittal he absconded and took up with some bushrangers. Lynch and two others were arrested for beating to death a convict called Smith. Smith had, it was alleged, been killed in retaliation for having testified against some bushrangers. Two of the three were hanged for the crime, but Lynch was acquitted, because, it seems, the main witness against him turned up at court too drunk to give coherent testimony.

About three years earlier, in 1832, 19-year-old Lynch had arrived in Sydney to serve a seven-year sentence for 'false pretences'. He worked in a chain gang in Sydney for a short time and was then assigned to a farm near Berrima. It was while working here that he made the acquaintance of a man called Mulligan, who, it seems from Lynch's account, had received stolen goods from him and had failed to pay for them. It was Mulligan's family that Lynch would later kill, partly in retaliation for this 'dishonesty'. Even though the goods were ill-gotten, Lynch saw them as his passport to leading an 'honest' life, and considered that Mulligan had betrayed him.

Lynch next helped himself to eight bullocks from a farm at Oldbury and began driving them to Sydney to sell. On the way, near the Razorback Mountain, he met up with a man called Ireland who, accompanied by an Aboriginal boy, was driving a cart of farm produce to Sydney for his employer, a Mr Cowper. Lynch, considering that the contents of the dray would bring more lucrative rewards than the bullocks, decided to appropriate them. They camped together overnight and at first light Lynch took the boy into the bush, ostensibly to help him round up the bullocks. Away from the camp he despatched the unsuspecting youngster with a single blow from a small axe. Returning to camp, he did the same for Ireland. He hid the bodies and went on his way, leaving the bullocks behind.

Not far from Sydney Cowper, the owner of the dray, met Lynch on the road and demanded an explanation. Lynch calmly and genially explained that he had met up with Ireland, who had been taken ill and who had asked Lynch to take charge of the dray. The boy had remained behind with Ireland. Cowper readily accepted the story and arranged to rendezvous with him in Sydney. Lynch hastened on, disposed of the produce, and got well clear of Sydney before Cowper arrived.

Lynch's next victims were a father and son team called Frazer. Lynch had driven Cowper's empty dray back to the area near Razorback Mountain, perhaps to find the abandoned bullocks, when he met up with the Frazers, who were driving a horsedrawn dray. They camped together and were joined by another cart and its occupants. Later in the evening, when they had settled for the night, they were awakened by a soldier who rode up and enquired about a stolen dray belonging to a Mr Cowper. He explained the circumstances of its theft and the murder of its drivers. Frazer senior, befuddled by sleep and perhaps by drink, did not make the obvious connection and sent the rider on his way.

Lynch, lying under the dray in question, overheard the exchange in considerable trepidation. He then plotted his future course.

Cowper's dray, if he stayed with it, would be his downfall. He accordingly decided to kill the Frazers and steal their dray and devised a plan for doing so. The next morning he went off early, supposedly to find the bullocks for his dray which he had unyoked the night before. He found them and chased them away. When he returned to the camp, only the Frazers remained. He told them his bullocks had strayed and could not be found. The Frazers, completely taken in, helped him conceal Cowper's dray in the bush and took him with them, presumably to search for the wandering bullocks. That night they camped again.

In the morning, the younger Frazer and Lynch went out to round up the horses. Saying that he felt cold, Lynch wore a jacket under which he concealed an axe. At an opportune moment he killed the 'young fellow' with a single blow. He took one horse back with him, and waited with Frazer senior for the son to bring in the other one. When, growing impatient, the older man turned to look for his son, Lynch swiftly felled him. He buried the bodies.

Carnage at Mulligan's farm

The killings and the disposal of the bodies had taken up much of the day and a good deal of Lynch's energy. He stayed that night at the scene of the crime. The next day he drove his newly acquired transport to the farm of his old acquaintance Mulligan, hoping to recoup the money that Mulligan owed him. Mulligan lived with a woman, not his wife but known as Mrs Mulligan, and her son and daughter, who were about 16 and 14 respectively.

Any suspicions he might have aroused were dispelled by telling them he was a hired driver. When he asked for payment for the stolen goods, Mrs Mulligan told him she did not have the money to hand. Nevertheless, Lynch decided to ingratiate himself with the Mulligans by plying them with some rum he bought at a nearby inn.

According to Lynch's confession, as the two adult Mulligans drank and he carefully avoided getting drunk, he brooded about Mulligan's treachery and the unfairness of his situation. He claimed that he prayed to Heaven for guidance on how to act and then felt that he saw his way clear to exact vengeance. In a bizarre variation of the ploy he used to kill young Frazer, Lynch used the cold as an excuse to lure the Mulligan boy outside to chop firewood. This time he had no need to conceal the axe. The unfortunate youth was an easy kill. Lynch, perhaps touched by some tinge of remorse as he faced his own imminent death, rationalised this murder by claiming to be morally outraged by the boy's conversation. The youngster, if we can believe Lynch, confided that he wished his father dead so that he could inherit the farm.

Back inside, Mrs Mulligan's suspicions were aroused when Lynch returned alone and the boy did not follow soon after. She asked Mulligan to fire off a gunshot to alert the boy to come home. Lynch objected that this might bring the police, hardly a reassuring reason for the increasingly anxious mother. Talking to Mulligan, he noticed Mrs Mulligan surreptitiously hand a carving knife to her daughter, indicating that she should conceal it in her dress. She then went out to look for her son.

Lynch was now desperate. He made some excuse to go out into the night. He located his axe and, meeting Mulligan hurrying after the woman, he struck him down. He had no trouble in similarly killing the woman.

Returning to the hut, he easily disarmed the now terrified young girl. Here, according to some accounts, he showed some grotesque semblance of humanity. During his confession, he temporarily lost his composure as he described how he murdered her. He explained to the distraught girl that he could not afford to leave her alive and gave her ten minutes to say her prayers. He then raped her and killed her with the axe. He dragged the four bodies together and contrived to set fire to them. He then buried what he could of the remains.

A masterful hoax

Lynch then perpetrated his greatest and cleverest hoax. He went to Sydney, where he placed a paid announcement in the *Sydney Gazette*, one of the two newspapers that were published in the colony, in Mulligan's name. This stated that Mrs Mulligan had left home and that Mulligan would not be responsible for any debts she may have incurred. He also wrote letters in Mulligan's name to various people in the neighbourhood—by looking through Mulligan's papers he had made himself very familiar with the man's business dealings and must have been able to make a fair job of copying his handwriting—informing them that he had sold the farm to a John Donleavy, the name under which Lynch lived on the farm. The master stroke was the letter he wrote to himself and had posted from another district. This purported to be from Mulligan to Donleavy and confirmed aspects of the imagined business arrangements between the two. He showed this around the local area as proof of his credentials and as a way of warding off any awkward questions. He even engaged former acquaintances of his, a married couple called Barnet, to work on the farm for him.

He lived for the next six months in relative prosperity, posing as a law-abiding local landholder and having no occasion or temptation to commit further murders. The drought was broken, however, one day when he was returning from a visit to Sydney. Camped once again near Razorback Mountain he fell in with a large man, Kearns Landregan, who claimed he had just separated from his wife and wished to live somewhere out of the way for some time. Lynch offered him a job doing fencing work on his farm and Landregan agreed.

The two set off together but on the way Landregan offended Lynch's moral sensitivities by describing how he cheated his wife of her money. Lynch's disapproval turned to disgust when, on passing a place where Landregan thought his wife was staying, he hid himself by lying down in the cart. Lynch became even more uneasy when some time later Landregan again hid, this time to avoid being seen by a man with whom he had quarrelled and whom he had taken to court. The man's seeming familiarity with the workings of the law, understandably enough, unsettled Lynch and may well have been the factor that decided him to add yet another victim to his tally. Such a man, especially one capable of cheating his wife, might soon sniff out his secret and would probably have no compunction about reporting him to the authorities.

Lynch's opportunity came the next morning, when Landregan was resting and smoking after chopping some firewood. Lynch seized Landregan's discarded tomahawk and knocked him down with all the force he could muster. Landregan was a large, powerfully built man and, in case the first blow had not fully achieved its purpose, Lynch administered a second one. This, according to Lynch's own account, was the first time he had ever struck a victim twice, and may have seemed an ominous sign.

It certainly seems to have unnerved him because, instead of disposing properly of the body, he merely hid it under a pile of freshly cut branches. This rather conspicuous mound, along with the gory remains that it barely concealed, was discovered the next day by a passing bullock driver. A series of clues, including grey horse hairs found near Lynch's and Landregan's camp site, led the investigation to Mulligan's farm, where one of the police identified the supposed Donleavy as the long-escaped convict John Lynch. The evidence that sealed Lynch's fate was Landregan's leather belt. Lynch had taken this home with him after throwing it into a waterhole and noticing that it was still visible. Given the ingenuity that had marked his criminal career up to this point, Lynch's carelessness on this occasion seems strange indeed.

A mere two days after committing his final atrocity, Lynch was arrested for the murder for which he would, two months later, be hanged.

William Westwood

A number of legends grew up around William Westwood, who was known popularly as Jackey Jackey. Like others before him, he acquired a reputation as a 'gentleman bushranger' and was known for his gallantry towards women and even his capacity for learned, 'grammatical' conversation. He was reported to have held his own on one occasion in a long, pleasant conversation with Sir George Gipps, governor of New South Wales from 1838 to 1846. However, it is hard to imagine how such an agreeable meeting could have occurred, as Westwood was, during the whole of that period, either a convict, a hunted bushranger with a price on his head, an escapee from captivity or a convicted felon serving a life sentence on Norfolk Island. It is also a little difficult to reconcile, at least at first sight, the violent and murderous rampage which led to Westwood's execution in October 1846 at the age of 26 with the imagery of romance with which popular accounts of his earlier exploits have been invested.

Westwood was the ringleader in a revolt on Norfolk Island that took place on 1 July 1846 and that left four of the prison officers dead, their heads crushed by axes and whatever other weapons the rioting prisoners had been able to get hold of. Westwood was directly responsible for at least one of these deaths.

Westwood's journey to Norfolk Island and to his death there on the gallows began almost ten years earlier. In 1837 the 16-year-old Westwood was transported to New South Wales to serve a seven-year sentence for petty theft. The education that the myth-makers later attributed to him is difficult to credit, given that the young offender had been a humble runner of errands before his conviction.

He was assigned to a farm near Goulburn where he spent almost three incident-free years. In late 1839 he made the first, and no doubt the easiest, of the numerous escapes from custody that characterised his career as an outlaw. He absconded and joined up for some time with another absconder, an unscrupulously brutal Irishman named Paddy Curran. The two held up numerous stations in the area, including the one to which Westwood had been assigned. In fact, the coming together of Westwood and Curran coincided with a minor epidemic of bushranging incidents in the Goulburn and Monaro areas. This no doubt helped fuel the stories that were later put about of Westwood's uncanny capacity to conduct hold-ups almost simultaneously in places that were impossibly distant from each other.

Westwood's association with Curran came to an end when Curran sexually assaulted a woman on a station that they were robbing. An infuriated Westwood, surprising Curran in the act, turned his gun on his accomplice and sent him off with neither horse, gun nor ammunition. Westwood's chivalry towards women thus became one of the key pieces in the jigsaw that was retrospectively assembled to represent his character.

Another important piece concerned the style and bravado of his exploits. He was reputed to be a horse thief of almost finicky discernment and a robber with an uncommonly fine taste in clothes. In one well-documented incident that occurred in May 1841, an elegantly attired Westwood rode up to a tollgate on the Parramatta Road, near the present Sydney University, and engaged the tollkeeper in conversation. He enquired of the unsuspecting official whether he knew of the whereabouts of the notorious Jackey Jackey Westwood and was informed that he was far away in the south. Westwood then revealed his identity but reassured the now alarmed man that he meant him no harm, revealing nevertheless the pistols that were concealed beneath his cloak. He also indicated that he had just substituted his tired old horse for a fresh one from nearby Grose's Farm. He then produced some money, suggesting that the tollkeeper go out and purchase them both some rum. The now bemused man explained that he could not leave his post, so Westwood himself rode off to a nearby inn, bought the rum and returned and shared it with his new-found companion before riding out of Sydney.

The death mask of William Westwood

This incident showed considerable daring, but its boldness was all the more marked for the fact that barely three months earlier Westwood had had a narrow and lucky escape from justice. In January 1841, following a spate of crimes that included several stagecoach hold-ups, robberies of lone travellers on country roads, a succession of horse thefts and a successful solo raid on a clothing and general provisions store, Westwood was spotted near Bungendore. He was pursued and surrounded by the local magistrate and several helpers and, after firing at his pursuers and missing, arrested at gunpoint and placed the local inn under guard. He escaped by seizing a gun from one of his guards and jumping through a window, only to be promptly recaptured by the magistrate's brother and another man.

This time his captors left nothing to chance. They tied him up and handed him over to a mounted policeman, Lieutenant Christie, who had been pursuing Westwood unsuccessfully for many weeks. Christie set out for Sydney with his prized prisoner, but along the way Westwood contrived to escape again. However, being unarmed and on foot, he was soon overtaken. He had to suffer the indignity of travelling for the rest of that day draped over and tied to a horse. That night the party reached Bargo and Westwood was placed in the local lock-up. From here, by means that are not clear—but the laxity and incompetence of his captors must have been a contributing factor—he escaped, complete with arms and ammunition. In a further act of effrontery, he staged a hold-up the next day, relieving his victim, a Mr Macarthur, of money and valuables as well as of his horse, which Westwood took in exchange for the inferior one he had managed to steal the previous evening.

The line between calculated bravado and carelessness can be a thin one. The actions that led to Westwood's next arrest smacked of both, especially considering the publicity that his previous escapes and the bounty of 30 pounds that was now offered for his apprehension, dead or alive, had engendered. Despite this, soon after his last brush with the law, Westwood went into an inn in Berrima, ordered some refreshments from the landlord's daughter and went into a back room where he reclined on a chair while he awaited service. The young woman recognized him and set up a commotion which brought both her parents and, unfortunately for Westwood, a nearby carpenter armed with a hammer, hurrying to investigate. It was the carpenter who effected the capture by felling the desperate young outlaw with a blow to the head.

Harsh conditions

Not surprisingly, Westwood was given a life sentence. He was confined, at first, to the gaol at Darlinghurst in Sydney. An escape attempt from here was foiled soon afterwards and Westwood was transferred to the grim penal establishment on Cockatoo Island, near Balmain, in Sydney Harbour. Here recalcitrant convicts were employed in the arduous task of hewing the island's sandstone to supply local building projects. From Cockatoo Island Westwood devised a plan of escape that seemed doomed to failure from the start. At the head of a gang of 25, he overcame and incapacitated a warder and plunged into the harbour, braving sharks and other hazards, to swim to Balmain. What plans they had beyond here are a matter for conjecture. Swift recapture seemed the most likely outcome. Even Balmain, however, proved too ambitious a goal. All 25 were picked up in the water and at their subsequent trial were sentenced to a term at Port Arthur in Van Diemen's Land. Here the gang arrived in a desperately weakened state, having been confined in an almost airless hold after staging an unsuccessful attempt to take control of the vessel that was transporting them to this place of dreaded punishment.

Undeterred by this string of failed escape attempts, Westwood refused to accept the fate that had been decreed for him. He broke out of Port Arthur, took to the bush and to outlawry again, but was soon recaptured. Since the end of George Arthur's stern and unyielding administration of the island in 1837, a less inflexible attitude to penal matters had prevailed under the governorship of Sir John Franklin. The pendulum, which had been securely wedged on the side of retribution, was now swinging more in the other direction, that of reformation. In Arthur's time so chronic a recidivist as Westwood would no doubt have been returned to harsher conditions at Port Arthur or disposed of forthwith on the gallows. Westwood, however, was sent instead to a less severe prison at Glenorchy, one intended to promote the rehabilitation of its inmates.

By now, though, he was beyond redemption. He escaped once more, was again recaptured, and this time sentenced to death, a sentence that was commuted to life imprisonment on Norfolk Island.

Norfolk Island

A convict settlement was set up on Norfolk Island soon after the founding of the colony in 1788, but it was abandoned in 1814. Eleven years later, under the governorship of Sir Ralph Darling, a prison was once again established there. It was to house only the most intractable of criminals and was designed to be a hell on earth, a place, as Governor Darling put it, 'of the extremest punishment short of Death'. Situated more than 1500 kilometres from Sydney in the South Pacific, it was virtually escape-proof, and its remoteness permitted the authorities to institute a regime of terror and cruelty that was not subject to regular scrutiny.

When, however, Westwood arrived on Norfolk Island, the prison there was under the administration of Captain Alexander Maconochie who for four years, from 1840 to 1844, put in place a series of humane reforms, designed to raise prisoner morale and encourage rehabilitation. Rewards rather than punishments were, albeit briefly, the order of the day; the gallows were demolished, the lash put to rest, and a system of 'marks'—to be awarded for productive work, or taken away for bad behaviour—was instituted in their place. Prisoners could exchange marks earned for time off their sentences or for other privileges. On his first day in charge, Maconochie pronounced a holiday, something previously unheard of in this place and which, when news of it reached Sydney, scandalised the many who were sceptical of or hostile to his ideas and hardened them against him. Maconochie was unique among colonial prison administrators in that he had experienced the miseries of harsh imprisonment and so undertood their corrosive effects. For two years, from the end of 1811, he had been a prisoner of war of the French.

Among the privileges that prisoners were allowed was the right to read books—Maconochie established a library of religious and other 'improving' books, including the works of Shakespeare—and to cook food in their cells. For this they were issued pots, pans and other utensils. They were also encouraged to tend their own vegetable plots, an innovation that helped to improve the standard of nutrition and to deter the epidemics of dysentery that had been a feature of life on the island.

Political opposition to such humanitarian treatment of the undeserving increased and by 1844 Lord Stanley, Secretary of State for the colonies, was prevailed upon to bring Maconochie's experiment to an end. Maconochie was recalled in January 1844 and replaced by the unimaginative disciplinarian, Major Joseph Childs, who immediately set about dismantling his predecessor's reforms.

Whether Westwood would have reformed under the continued regime of Maconochie and eventually, like his fellow prisoner, Martin Cash, been granted his freedom, we will never know. In the months after Childs took over, prisoner morale plummeted, the lash and the gallows made their reappearance and, when these failed to subdue the insubordinate, a range of cruel tortures, including confinement for days on end in a small cells half filled with water, was instituted. A spirit of resentment and barely supressed revolt prevailed among the prisoners.

The uprising

The incident that gave rise to the riot in July 1846 was, ironically, not directly attributable to any of Childs' harsh measures. More than two years after taking charge of the prison, he had still not removed the prisoners' rights to cook in their cells. However, on 30 June, William Forster, the official in charge of stores, suspecting that many cooking utensils and provisions were being pilfered, gathered up as many as he could find after the prisoners had been locked up for the night and locked them in a storeroom in order to take an inventory.

The next morning a group of prisoners, finding their possessions missing, stormed the storeroom and recovered them, then proceeded to make their breakfast. But the anger had not subsided and a little later, a large group, led by Westwood, let out a rallying cry. They were soon joined by the majority of the prisoners who, taking the guards by surprise, went on their destructive rampage. The attack, a spontaneous outpouring of pent-up fury, was directed towards a hated magistrate called Barrow and the mob surged towards his house, killing whoever sought to bar their progress. It had, of course, no chance of success. When they had recovered from the initial shock, the soldiers soon herded the rioters at gun and bayonet point back into the prison's lumber yard.

Westwood's fate was a foregone conclusion. He and 13 others were put on trial as ringleaders of the revolt. Twelve of the 14 were sentenced to death after a trial that allowed the prisoners to present no defence and in which only prosecution witnesses were called. There is some suspicion that at least some of the accused took no leading role in the riot, but were known troublemakers on whom the authorities took the opportunity to exact revenge. In a final declaration, written just before his execution, Westwood named four of the condemned as being innocent of the crimes of which they were accused. One of them was Lawrence Kavanagh, the former associate of Martin Cash. Westwood's statement, though, made no difference. The 12 condemned men were hanged, in two groups of six, on 13 October 1846.

Cash's former reviled associate, Paddy Curran, had suffered a similar fate five years earlier. In 1841 he was convicted of a murder and a rape committed near Bungendore. Although he was not tried for them, he was also accused of several other murders and at least one other rape.

Edward Davis

The year 1841 also saw the public hanging of another bushranger, but one whose exploits had attracted a great deal more public sympathy than did Paddy Curran's. In scenes that were reminiscent of Matthew Brady's execution in Hobart just under 15 years earlier, Edward Davis was publicly hanged in Sydney, along with six of his accomplices. Soldiers had to restrain the large, emotional crowd, many of whom volubly expressed their support for the convicted felons. Known popularly as the 'Jew-boy', Davis absconded from a chain gang early in 1839 and was, for almost two years, the terror of the roads in the Hunter and New England districts. His reported adventures—real, imagined and no doubt often highly embellished—caught the public imagination. His appeal, like that of Matthew Brady, derived largely from his manifest contempt for established authority and the opportunities he took on several occasions to ridicule it and avenge its tyrannies.

In one widely reported incident, he and his gang laid hold of a convict overseer on a property near Scone. They took him out into the bush and convened a court which tried the unfortunate man for his supposed mistreatment of his convict labourers. He was, of course, found guilty and was sentenced to three dozen lashes, which were duly administered on the spot. In another, he

After they were hanged, Westwood and his fellow mutineers were buried in a disused sawpit. The unmarked earth that was heaped on top became known as 'Murders' Mound'. It is no longer visible today.

and his men turned the tables on a police party, led by the chief constable of the district, who had been sent out in search of them. The outlaws lay in wait for their pursuers, then fell upon them and relieved them of their weapons, horses and money. On another occasion the gang raided a hotel, bailed up two policemen who were drinking there and forced them at gunpoint to drink themselves insensible. These supposed upholders of the law were roundly condemned in a Sydney newspaper which reported the incident for the apparent relish with which they complied with the bushrangers' instructions.

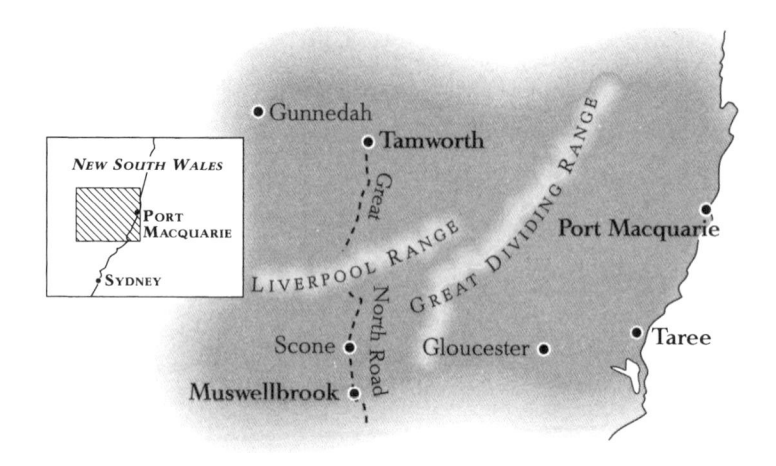

It is probable that many of the robberies that were attributed to Davis and his gang were in fact committed by other less well-known bushrangers or by former members of his gang. Membership of the gang was fluid, although the six that were hanged with Davis seem to have constant colleagues in crime; its numbers fluctuated as new absconders joined or others, weary of the privations of outlaw life, surrendered to authorities and took their punishment. Less than six months after Davis bolted, four of his accomplices were captured and hanged.

Despite this and other setbacks, Davis had virtual control of the lonely roads that linked the developing centres of population to the north and north-west of Sydney. During 1839 and 1840 lone travellers ventured along them at their peril, although the bushrangers rarely mistreated them, apart from taking their horses, money and valuables. They also frequently raided homesteads, stations (especially to steal horses) and mail coaches. After one mail coach robbery one of the gang made off with most of the proceeds and lived on them in Sydney for some time until he was recognised and arrested.

The gang set up a headquarters at a place in the Liverpool Ranges called Doughboy Hollow. From this elevated position they could monitor the traffic on the Great North Road that led to the recently established village of Tamworth. It is probable that the gang established friendly relations with the local Aboriginal people, who may well have kept them informed of the whereabouts of the search parties that were sent with increasing frequency to find them. It was widely believed that an Aboriginal woman lived with Davis in his hideout and often accompanied the gang on its raids.

Towards the end of 1840, Davis and his gang held up a store in Scone. As they helped themselves to the provisions, a young storeman, John Graham, opened fire on the robbers and ran to alert the local police. Graham's shots did not find their mark, but the aim of John Shea was more certain. As Graham hurried away a shot from Shea's gun struck him dead. It was the first murder the gang had committed.

After this incident the hunt intensified. Finally, in December 1840, a raid on the house of a Captain Horsley not far from Maitland, in which the captain and his wife were forced to lie in bed while the robbers ransacked the house and verbally abused them, so insensed local magistrate and Waterloo veteran, Edward Day, that he immediately gathered a search party of soldiers and volunteers. The heavily armed group headed along the Great Northern Road and on 23 December, just two days after the assault on Horsley's house, they tracked down the gang, which now consisted of only its seven hard-core members, near their hideout. In the fight that ensued, Davis was wounded and he and five of his accomplices were forced to surrender. One man, Richard Glanville, escaped but was caught the next day.

As we noted earlier, the system of convict transportation created the conditions in which bushranging flourished. In 1840 transportation to New South Wales ceased, and as the influx of resentful, alienated young lawbreakers dwindled, there was a corresponding decline in the incidence of bushranging throughout the colony. The downfall of Westwood and Davis did not spell the end of bushranging for the time being—there were sporadic outbreaks during the rest of the decade—but their careers did represent the last spectacular manifestations of convict revolt. The next major outbreak would usher in what is often referred to, rather ambiguously, as the 'golden age of bushranging'.

THE EUREKA GANG AND CAPTAIN MELVILLE
Bushrangers of the Victorian Goldfields

In April 1851 gold was found at Ophir near Bathurst in central western New South Wales. Just four months later another find was made, this time near the present town of Ballarat in the newly independent colony of Victoria. These events gave rise to a series of goldrushes and, in turn, a succession of new outbreaks of bushranging. The goldrushes resulted in the rapid development of ramshackle new settlements in parts of the country where there was no infrastructure, where the most rapid form of communication was a rider on horseback and where the maintenance of law and order, at least in the early stages, was either non-existent or rudimentary and haphazard.

Conditions of life on the goldfields constituted a perfect recipe for anarchy. Men, many of whom had been scarred by the depression of the 1840s and lured by the hope, usually frustrated, of making a quick fortune, lived in close proximity to each other in unsanitary makeshift dwellings. Tensions and jealousies were rife, especially as hopefuls from further afield, many of them speaking unknown tongues and of alien appearance and culture, arrived to swell the diggers' numbers (as early as April 1852 it was estimated that there were 30 000 men prospecting for gold in Victoria). These antagonisms often erupted into violence and murders which frequently remained unsolved or even undetected.

A digger was likely to be in conflict, not only with his neighbours, but also with the police and other authorities who sought, often enough ineptly and insensitively, to impose an orderly regime on the mayhem of the goldfields. Another worry was bushrangers—those entrepreneurial outlaws who sensed,

The Eureka Gang and Captain Melville

V. R.

Chief Secretary's Office,
Melbourne, 8th July, 1857.

WILFUL MURDER.

£50 REWARD.

WHEREAS the HEAD of a MURDERED FEMALE has been found at the bottom of a hole situated in an abandoned gully known by the name of "*Paddy's Gully*," a mile and a half from the township of Avoca, and in a neighbouring hole in the same locality a piece of canvas stained with blood has also been found: And whereas a skeleton without a head, and otherwise dismembered, with an axe lying alongside, has been discovered on an open piece of ground about four miles from the said gully: And whereas the said human remains are supposed to have belonged to the same individual: Notice is hereby given that a Reward of FIFTY POUNDS will be paid to any person who shall give such information as will lead to the apprehension and conviction of the person or persons who murdered the said female.

By His Excellency's Command,

WILLIAM C. HAINES.

PARTICULARS.

On Monday, 15th June, one of two miners working in an abandoned gully called "*Paddy's Gully*," 1½ miles from Avoca, found the head of a European female at the bottom of a hole. The head was fractured in two places. It had been severed from the trunk by a sharp instrument. At the top of the forehead there is a bullet hole. The teeth are entire, except two, which are decayed. Some reddish brown hair lay beside the head. The deceased is supposed to have been about 30 years of age, and to have been dead about three months or more.

In a neighbouring hole had been previously found a tarpaulin or a canvas fly covered with blood: it appears to be a dray cover. The skeleton was found on an open piece of ground near the Four mile flat (on Mr. Bradshaw's run), it is destitute of the head, and otherwise incomplete. An American axe, rusted with blood, with a straight handle of iron bark, lay alongside the skeleton.

The murder appears to have been committed while the parties were camped for the night, and the head was carried four miles from the trunk in a direction leading up the country towards Avoca.

By Authority: John Ferres, Government Printer, Melbourne.

Evidence of lawlessness on the Victorian goldfields

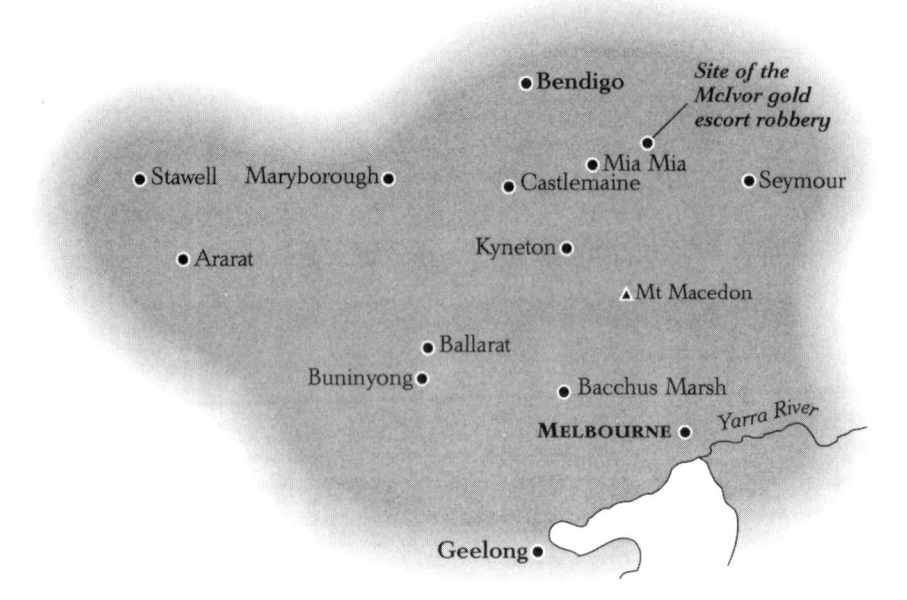

rightly for the most part, but almost always to their own ultimate cost—that here was a situation that was ripe for exploitation.

The first major outbreaks of bushranging in the wake of gold discoveries occurred in Victoria. This was at least partly because of the proximity of the Victorian goldfields to Tasmania where there were many convicts and former convicts only too willing to take up the challenges and the opportunities that gold promised.

It was assumed, probably too glibly, that the new and burgeoning spate of robberies and hold-ups was entirely the work of refugees from the island colony. The new breed of outlaws who operated on the roads leading to and from the diggings were variously referred to as 'Derwenters', 'Vandemonians' and 'Tothersiders'. Melbourne and Geelong gaols were soon unable to cope with the new influx of wrongdoers; new gaols were established at Ballarat and Bendigo and early in 1853 two old ships, the *President* and the *Success*, were pressed into service as convict hulks.

The growing prison population included, along with captured bushrangers and other offenders, those diggers who had proved unable or unwilling to pay the licence fees that the governor of Victoria, Charles Latrobe, had decreed

The prison hulk Success, *from which McCallum made his unsuccessful, but murderous, escape bid.*

that all miners should pay. One common complaint of the miners, often echoed in the press, was that the police were too obsessed with harassing them about licence fees to be effective in deterring more serious crimes. In March 1853, the *Geelong Advertiser* took the Victorian government to task for failing to prevent 'the robberies, assaults, and murders committed by bushrangers upon a number of luckless wayfarers, with the grossest and most notorious impunity' along the roads leading to the diggings. It dismissed the defence that the area in need of protection was too great to be patrolled, citing the success of New South Wales in patrolling its goldfield roads.

A bill that forbade entry to Victoria by Tasmanian convicts became law late in 1852, but was largely ineffective as wily convicts easily enough escaped detection at entry ports or sailed to Sydney and then came overland to the new colony. The police, despite the complaints against them, were reasonably successful in bringing bushrangers to justice. The police in Victoria, which had previously been a rather ad hoc group with no centralised control, was re-formed in 1853 under the leadership of a chief commissioner and with a graded ranking system. By early 1854 it had grown to number just over 2000 men. Some of them were 'imported' from England, but the majority were recruited locally, largely from the ranks of disenchanted gold diggers. By about the middle of the decade the police had largely brought the gold-inspired bushranging outbreak under control.

Some idea of the magnitude of the law and order situation can be gauged from the fact that at the beginning of 1853, 90 prisoners were awaiting trial in Melbourne for offences punishable by death. The first of the new breed of Victorian bushrangers infested the roads that led north and along which many people were travelling on their way to the diggings near Bathurst in New South Wales. Later, after the first Victorian gold discoveries, successful prospectors, rich with earnings from their finds and, for those willing to take greater risks, the heavily guarded gold escorts that brought large amounts of gold to Melbourne, provided richer pickings.

Early in 1852 a gang of four 'Vandemonians' virtually commandeered one of the roads out of Bendigo for three days, amassing a total of 33 pounds of gold. Their greed for gold was clearly stronger than their good sense; they continued their depredations until a contingent of mounted police arrived, who shot one of them dead and pursued and captured the other three, who fled to a nearby hotel.

In late 1852 a gang of five, led by John Finegan and John Donovan, and known as the Eureka gang, were apprehended in a hotel at Buninyong, near where the first Victorian gold find was made. They were brought to trial for a series of robberies that took place over a wide area, and that bore similar hallmarks. These robbers subjected the people they bailed up to the indignity of being stripped and searched for any concealed money or valuables. Despite being identified in court by their aggrieved victims, the accused claimed that they could not have committed the crimes attributed to them, given that some were alleged to have occurred almost simultaneously in locations distant from each other. This defence cut no ice with an unsympathetic jury and the gang members were sentenced to prison for terms of either six or 12 years.

The McIvor gold escort robbery

One of the most notorious bushranging events of the decade was the hold-up and robbery of the escort bringing gold from the McIvor goldfield to Kyneton in July 1853. Three armed troopers were with the driver on the cart bearing the gold and another policeman and the escort leader were mounted on horses. As the cart approached a sharp bend, it was forced to veer to one side of the road to avoid a log that was blocking the way. While the driver was negotiating this obstacle, shots rang out from the bushes, mortally wounding the driver and also injuring the three troopers. The two mounted horses were also hit. In the confusion that followed, a group of men ran to the cart, seized the two boxes of gold, worth 5000 pounds, and made off with them, leaving their horses behind. The escort leader, whose name was Warner, managed to ride his injured horse to a nearby station and summon help. When he arrived back, he found a passer-by, whom he at first mistakenly thought to be one of the robbers, tending the injured troopers and driver. There was no sign of the bushrangers or the gold, except for three abandoned horses nearby in the bush. The driver, Thomas Flooks, died soon afterwards.

Some months passed and the crime remained unsolved until a John Murphy was arrested on board a ship about to set sail for England. He confessed his part in the event and, to avoid punishment, he informed on his fellow robbers,

The attack on the McIvor gold escort

one of whom was his brother, Jeremiah Murphy, who had fled to Queensland. Jeremiah was tracked down and he too bought his freedom by revealing the whereabouts of the other gang members—George Wilson, George Atkins and George Melville—who were subsequently arrested, tried and hanged. In a macabre twist, the execution was botched: Wilson and Melville's necks failed to break as they dropped through the trap and the two men writhed in agony at the end of their ropes. Before this, John Murphy, smitten with remorse or fear, had taken his own life.

The short and turbulent career of Captain Melville

The nature of their career condemned the majority of bushrangers to an early death, usually at the end of a rope. The most noted bushranger of the Victorian goldfields era died young, although his age is not known for certain, and he died by strangulation, but by a scarf rather than a rope. On 10 August 1857, Frank McCallum, known generally as Captain Melville, was found dead in his cell in Melbourne's Pentridge Prison. Officially death was decreed to have been self-inflicted, although there is a strong suspicion that he was strangled by a prison warder in retribution for an attack that McCallum, who was given to violent and uncontrollable rages, had made on the prison's governor just under two weeks earlier.

Less than a year before this McCallum had been sentenced to the gallows for the murder of a prison officer during an escape attempt. McCallum who, at that time, was being held aboard the convict hulk *Success* in Hobson's Bay, was, along with about 50 other prisoners, being towed in a barge towards the quarry where they were to work. The prisoners attempted to overpower the towing vessel and escape. In this unsuccessful bid for freedom, McCallum, it seems, had killed a Corporal Owen with a hammer.

The sentence of death that was passed was subsequently commuted and McCallum was moved to Pentridge. His killing of Owen was widely held to have inspired the murder of John Price, the inspector-general of convicts in Victoria and the man who had succeeded, and continued the brutal regime of, Major Childs on Norfolk Island. In March 1857 Price was surrounded and stoned and battered to death by prisoners from the *Success* when he visited the quarry at Williamstown for which McCallum had been bound before the abortive escape attempt. Price's death was supposed by many to have been planned by McCallum.

When he died, McCallum, alias Captain Melville, had been in custody for more than four years. The notoriety that had surrounded his career as Victoria's most wanted bushranger had long since subsided.

McCallum's pre-bushranging history remains largely a matter of speculation. He is variously supposed to have been an ex-convict from Van Diemen's Land who had been transported as a petty criminal in 1838, or to have arrived in the colony as a free immigrant and to have tried his hand unsuccessfully at gold digging before taking to the roads as an outlaw. During 1852, in association with William Roberts, he carried out a series of robberies and had a price on his head.

About a week before Christmas he and Roberts staged a much-publicised raid on a sheep station near Wardy Yallock owned by a man called Aitcheson. Aitcheson and 17 of his staff were bailed up at pistol point by the two intruders and were left ignominiously roped to a fence while McCallum and Roberts systematically ransacked the house, herded the women into a room, helped themselves to food and alcohol, as well as to two of the station's best horses, and then went on their way. The sheer audacity of the exercise earned McCallum a kind of grudging admiration.

Over the next few days the two bandits moved towards Geelong, staging as they went a series of hold-ups which netted them both money and gold. On one occasion they held up a pair of diggers who were going on holidays with the proceeds of their goldfield earnings; the bandits returned part of their takings so that their victims could still enjoy their Christmas break.

Whether the two diggers managed to celebrate Christmas with their reduced resources we cannot know. For McCallum and Roberts, however, Christmas was decidedly disastrous. On Christmas eve, they arrived in the town of Geelong where they first put up at a hotel and then went to visit a nearby brothel. With his senses lulled by a generous intake of alcohol, and his ego flattered by the tender ministrations of the prostitutes, McCallum carelessly bragged about his exploits and even revealed his identity. The women, whose commercial sense was by no means dimmed, and who knew of the 100 pounds reward offered for McCallum's capture, contrived to keep him occupied while one of them went for the police. Perhaps something in their manner alerted McCallum to the peril, for he abruptly left the premises just in time to avoid apprehension, leaving the now thoroughly drunken Roberts to the mercies of the police.

Unable to get to his horse, McCallum made his way across the town with the police not far behind. He came across a young man who was quietly riding a horse, seized him by the leg and brought him to the ground. The frightened horse, however, reared dangerously as McCallum tried to mount and the young man was able to grab his adversary and wrestle with him, until the police, following the sounds of the disturbance, arrived and seized the outlaw.

George Boxall, who half a century later wrote a history of Australian bushranging, was a boy in Geelong when the notorious Melville was arrested and was part of the crowd that gathered to see him and Roberts conveyed from the gaol to the courthouse to stand trial. In his description of the scene, the two bushrangers 'were seated in a dray, heavily ironed … and drawn by two horses. There were several armed policemen on the dray, and others marched before and behind. The courthouse, of course, was crowded, and, as boys were not admitted, I was not present.'

The verdict, of course, was guilty on each of the three charges of highway robbery. McCallum was sentenced to a total of 32 years imprisonment, although as the terms were to be served concurrently, this effectively meant 12 years. He was sent first to the prison hulk *President* in Hobson's Bay, as a place of very severe punishment. Some time later, presumably because he had behaved tractably, he was transferred to the *Success*, where conditions were generally less grim. Subsequent events, however, were to prove that he remained far from chastened.

FRANK GARDINER
New Outbreaks in New South Wales

While the New South Wales goldrushes of the 1850s did not generate the level of lawlessness that broke out in the wake of the Victorian gold discoveries, the areas around the diggings were by no means free of trouble. In 1853, for example, a Bathurst newspaper graphically catalogued a number of brutal murders that had occurred in the area, denouncing the authorities for their apparent inability to prevent or solve them. Much of this violence, however, was random and could not be attributed to any individual or gang. It certainly did not constitute an outbreak of bushranging.

This situation changed dramatically in the early 1860s. The catalyst, at least in part, for this renewal of organised, systematic outlawry was a series of disturbances and riots which occurred at Lambing Flat in 1860 and 1861. Lambing Flat was on the Burrangong goldfield which had been discovered in March 1860 near the site of the present town of Young. At least three of the great identities of Australian bushranging—Frank Gardiner, Ben Hall and Johnny Gilbert— were in the vicinity of Lambing Flat at the time of the disturbances and were able to observe the impotence of the law-enforcing authorities.

The tensions that are inevitable in any frontier situation were exacerbated at Lambing Flat by racial ones. The rich promise of the Burrangong goldfield attracted large numbers, including many Chinese. Not surprisingly the Chinese formed a separate group and their alien appearance, dress, language, food, habits—including that of smoking opium rather than consuming alcohol—and religious observances, as well as their dedication to the task of finding gold, aroused the suspicion and ire of the European miners. Troubles began almost immediately. A number of more or less violent attacks on the Chinese culminated on 30 June 1861 when, in a frenzy of xenophobic hatred, a mob of more than 2000 European diggers, armed with pickaxes, whips and whatever other weapons they could lay their hands on, and many of them well primed with liquor, swarmed over the Chinese camp, destroying and looting and driving more than 1000 distressed Chinese to take refuge on a nearby station. While all this was taking place, a small police contingent stood helplessly by.

Two weeks later, three men were arrested for their role as ringleaders in the riot, but on the same night a large mob of miners attacked the police, causing them to retreat from the goldfield until reinforcements could be brought up from Sydney at the end of July. For about two weeks, then, there was no law enforcement at Lambing Flat.

The chaos that prevailed for so long at Lambing Flat sent messages to those on both sides of the law. To the Gardiners, Halls and Gilberts it signalled that they could flout, or continue to flout, the law with relative impunity; and to the authorities it finally brought home the fact that the law and order situation was in urgent need of reform. Bushranging in western New South Wales was also on the increase at that time and the dangers posed to travellers to and from the goldfields by Frank Gardiner and his partner John Peisley further highlighted the ineffectiveness of the police.

In March 1862 the disparate elements of the New South Wales police force were brought under a single authority, as the Victorian police had been almost a decade earlier. At the head of the force was an inspector general—the first one, and the man who devised the system—Captain John McLerie. He remained in the job until he died in 1874 and received a posthumous award for the part he played in putting down the bushranging threat. There were nine ranks below that of inspector general, ranging downwards from superintendents to constables. The colony was divided into nine divisions, each one under the control of a superintendent. The goldfields came under the jurisdiction of the Western Division, which had its headquarters in Bathurst.

The former muzzle-loading rifles and single-shot pistols with which the police were issued were replaced under the new system by breech-loading rifles and six-shot hand guns. In spite of this reorganisation and the superior armaments, bushranging was rife in country areas for most of the decade. Part of the problem lay in the smallness of police numbers; the entire force consisted of

Frank Gardiner

Barely two months after these new arrangements were put in place, the force suffered an enormous blow to its morale and its reputation. On 15 June 1862, a gang under the leadership of Frank Gardiner staged the biggest robbery so far undertaken in the colony, that of the Forbes gold escort, bearing a total of 14 000 pounds worth in gold and money from Forbes to Orange.

When Gardiner and his gang, which at this stage included Ben Hall and Johnny Gilbert, pulled off this coup, Gardiner was already 32 years old and had a long history of bushranging and other acts of outlawry. He was commonly known as 'Darkie', often referred to himself as 'Prince of Tobymen' and 'King of the Road', and went in different places and at different times under the names of Frank Clark and Frank Christie. The title 'Darkie', first bestowed on him by Jack Newton, one of his early partners in crime, referred both to his long black hair, which he wore at shoulder length, and to his swarthy complexion. Clark and Christie, according to some accounts, were the names of his mother and father respectively.

Legend has it that Gardiner was the product of an affair between Charles Christie, a Scottish emigrant who supervised convict labour on a station near Goulburn, and Annie Clark, a servant of Irish and Aboriginal descent. According to this version, the affair ended when Christie's wife followed him to New South Wales

This sketch of Frank Gardiner in his prime, taken from a contemporary photograph, is an excellent likeness.

and young Frank grew up as the son of the two Christies. It has also been claimed that Christie and his wife arrived in Sydney in 1834 with five children, ranging in age from 12 months to ten years, of which five-year-old Frank was one. At the age of 10, the young boy ran away from home and worked on a farm for about three years. When he was only 13 he took up with a gang of horse thieves who operated under the cover of the Abercrombie Ranges, about 70 kilometres south of Bathurst.

In 1850 Gardiner, known at this stage as Frank Christie, was arrested, along with Jack Newton and another associate called Bill Troy, in a hotel near Ballarat. Gardiner, who was, strangely enough given his background, literate, had forged a letter to a local trader to whom the trio was trying to sell some stolen horses. Troy escaped before being brought to trial but Gardiner and Newton were sentenced to five years in Pentridge Prison. About a year later Gardiner escaped and took to bushranging around the Victorian goldfields.

In 1854 he was back in the Abercrombie region, now as Francis Clarke, living with, and in criminal partnership with, an old acquaintance and accomplished horse and cattle thief, William Fogg. Fogg and his wife lived in a simple slab hut in a remote location on the Fish River not far from the settlement of Bigga. Against Fogg's advice, Gardiner drove a number of stolen horses to Yass to sell to a horse dealer there, but the dealer became suspicious about the forged documents that Gardiner presented to prove ownership of the merchandise. The brash but careless young Gardiner had forged them in full view of onlookers as he drank at a local inn. The dealer went to the police, and for the second time Gardiner, with an associate, was arrested as he slept in a local hotel, waiting for his business to be completed.

This time he was sent to Sydney's Cockatoo Island to serve seven years' hard labour. Despite one failed attempt at escape, Gardiner was released at the end of 1859 on a ticket-of-leave and sent to Carcoar, where he worked for some time for a local butcher. However, still unchastened by his brushes with justice, he soon ceased reporting to the authorities—a condition of his release—and returned to his lawless ways. He went back to Fogg's hut and this time, in league with his host, took to cattle duffing.

In 1860 he turned up at the Lambing Flat diggings running a butcher shop in which he sold the carcasses of stolen cattle. His shop became a gathering point for some of the most desperate and rebellious elements on the goldfields and it was not long before the source of his merchandise came to the notice of the authorities. Early in 1861, Gardiner, who was still going under the name of Clarke, was arrested, but when he was released on bail he made for the hills. Here he met up with John Peisley, a former horse thief and now a wanted bushranger whom Gardiner had first met while doing time on Cockatoo Island. Together, and in collaboration with other refugees from justice, they staged hold-ups over a wide area that ranged from Bathurst to Lambing Flat (now Young) and as far south as Yass and Gundagai. This association was cut short, however, when Peisley was arrested in March 1862 for the murder of an innkeeper near the town of Bigga. He was hanged the following month.

A narrow escape

Not long after his escape and soon after his association with Peisly began, Gardner came close to being brought once again to justice. The police had received information that Gardiner (he was now going under the name Frank Gardiner) was hiding out with Fogg. On 15 July 1861 Sergeant John Middleton, accompanied by a trooper, William Hosie, and disguised as travellers but with arms concealed under their capes, set out on horseback from Bigga bound for Fogg's place. Middleton also had with him a riding whip, the handle of which was weighted with lead and would itself serve as a potentially lethal weapon.

They reached Fish River the next day and on approaching and entering the hut, Middleton noticed a movement behind a screen that divided the interior into two rooms. He drew his revolver and challenged Gardiner, who had indeed retreated behind the screen, to come out. Both Gardiner and Middleton fired simultaneously; Middleton's bullet grazed the side of Gardiner's head, stunning but not seriously wounding him. Gardiner's, on the other hand, hit Middleton in the mouth. Middleton managed to pull the trigger once again, but his gun failed to fire. Gardiner fired two more shots, hitting his adversary in the hand and the hip. At this point, Hosie came into the hut, firing wildly at Gardiner but missing him by a wide margin. Gardiner's answering shot brought Hosie down with a wound to the temple.

A struggle then ensued between Gardiner and Middleton who, despite his injuries, remained on his feet and managed a blow to Gardiner's head with his weighted whip handle. Hosie, too, recovered his balance and the two policemen managed to subdue Gardiner and handcuff him. Meanwhile the Foggs stood helplessly by.

Weakened from loss of blood and in great pain, Middleton nevertheless set out on horseback for Bigga to gather reinforcements, leaving Hosie to guard Gardiner. Both Gardiner and Hosie later gave conflicting versions of what happened next. According to Gardiner, while Hosie was momentarily distracted, he, handcuffed as he was, grabbed the trooper by the neck, bringing him down and forcing him to drop his gun. A furious struggle ensued in which Hosie fired again and missed. Eventually, Fogg, fearing for the consequences to himself of a renewed struggle and anxious to avoid having a dead policeman found on his premises, offered Hosie 50 pounds to let Gardiner go and say he escaped.

This sketch of Johnny Gilbert appeared in the Illustrated Melbourne Post *in June 1865.*

Hosie's story depicts him in a more heroic light. He claims that after the struggle, from which he emerged the victor, he had waited for some time for Middleton's reinforcements to appear. When no-one came, he had set out, with Fogg, to take Gardiner to Bigga. On the way, however, they were waylaid by Peisley and another of Gardiner's associates called Johnny Gilbert. Whatever really happened, it is certain that Hosie arrived in Bigga by himself, to be followed some time later by Middleton who, more dead than alive, had become lost on the way.

Not surprisingly, Hosie's version was accepted and Gardiner's arrest and subsequent liberation by his cohorts became widely talked about. This prompted Peisley to send a letter to a Bathurst newspaper, indignantly denying any part in the affair and also claiming, for good measure, that he had never used violence against any of his victims and had never shown rudeness to a woman.

Peisley's assertion was not widely credited, especially as just a bare two months later he shot and mortally wounded an innkeeper after wounding his brother and then threatening to kill a servant girl who stood between him and his victim. However, even on the scaffold, Peisley strongly asserted his lack of involvement in Gardiner's rescue.

Both Middleton and Hosie survived their wounds, but the incident increased the pressure on the police, from public and press alike, to bring the miscreant Gardiner to justice. Gardiner, too, now a mature man of more than 30, with a strongly developed sense of survival, took stock of the situation. As well, he had formed a liaison with a young woman, Catherine Brown, the wife of John Brown, a stockman employed by John McGuire, who ran a property in conjunction with Ben Hall. McGuire had married Ellen Walsh, and Hall her sister Bridget. Catherine was the younger sister of Ellen and Bridget. Gardiner had, then, a kind of de facto relationship with Ben Hall, who at this stage was no outlaw but who would soon become Gardiner's successor as the most wanted bushranger in New South Wales.

Gardiner decided to quit the local scene for a while. He made his temporary farewells to Catherine—Kate to him—and went for some time to South Australia.

Sir Frederick Pottinger

The man who bore much of the brunt of the public demand for more effective policing in western New South Wales was Sir Frederick Pottinger, who in October 1861 was promoted to the rank of inspector and given charge of policing in the southern district, based in Forbes, of the New South Wales Western Division. The pursuit and defeat of Frank Gardiner, then, became his immediate obsession.

Pottinger had both the advantage and disadvantage of being the son of an Irish baronet and of inheriting his title. He arrived in Australia in 1856, roughly simultaneously with his father's death, and joined the police force as a trooper. He had been a lieutenant in the Grenadier Guards for four years, but had to sell his commission after he gambled away most of his considerable fortune. He was a devotee of the racetrack and seems to have left England to escape his debtors. His rapid promotion in the New South Wales police force, despite his relative lack of experience and unfamiliarity with bush conditions, was a prime example of colonial cultural cringe: it would hardly do to have a baronet serving as a low-ranking policeman! On the other hand, colonials would be only too ready to criticise any apparent failures or incompetencies of such a man. In Pottinger's favour it must be asserted that he appears not to have used his baronetcy in order to further his cause; he joined the force as Frederick Pottinger and it was only by chance some time that later his aristocratic connections became known.

As it turned out, Pottinger, although he faltered spectacularly on several occasions, probably proved more effective than otherwise in the anti-bushranging cause. His relentless, if sometimes rather clumsy, efforts succeeded in bringing a number of offenders to justice, and there is no doubting his physical courage. And although a narrowly failed late-night ambush of Frank Gardiner as he visited Kate Brown made Pottinger the butt of innumerable lewd jokes and the subject of widespread ridicule, it was no doubt largely responsible for the bushranger's eventual retirement from the local scene.

Back on the scene

By early 1862 Gardiner was well and truly back in New South Wales. As well as holding up a number of rural properties, he was reportedly responsible for, if not personally present at, a much-publicised robbery of two storekeepers from the settlements of Wombat and Little Wombat near Lambing Flat. In this outrage four bushrangers relieved the unfortunate men, Horsington and Hewitt, of gold and money to the value of almost 2000 pounds. This robbery was mentioned in a letter, perhaps of dubious authenticity, from Gardiner which was published in the *Lachlan Miner* in April 1862. In it, Gardiner defended himself of charges, which had been reported in newspapers, that he had been guilty of petty theft from victims of his robberies. He also claimed that a gun that had discharged during the robbery of Horsington and Hewitt had been fired in error and that the man responsible had been sacked from his gang. If it was authentic, the letter read like an attempt to shore up support for him and his like in the face of rising public anger against the bushranging menace.

In April 1862, Ben Hall was arrested at a race meeting in Forbes on the orders of Sir Frank Pottinger. He was charged with being an accomplice of Frank Gardiner in the robbery of a cart driver about two weeks earlier. Hall, it seems, had been present at the robbery but may well have taken no active part in it. According to an account later given by his partner and brother-in-law, John McGuire, Hall had been riding along in company with his stockman when they had been joined unexpectedly by Gardiner. When they met the cart further along, Gardiner drew his gun and bailed up its driver.

When the case came to court in Orange in May, Hall was acquitted when the driver failed to positively identify him as being present at the hold-up. Even before this incident, Hall was a deeply embittered man; his wife, Bridget, had recently run off with another local landowner, James Taylor, taking with her the couple's two-year-old son. Now this brush with the law increased his feelings of alienation. When Gardiner visited Hall to apologise for implicating him in the crime, Hall, according to McGuire, swore that next time 'they'll have something to take me for'.

Robbery at Eugowra Rocks

Next time was not long in coming. In an attack that was reminiscent of Frank McCallum's robbery of the McIvor gold escort just under nine years earlier, a gang of eight, led by Gardiner and including Ben Hall, waylaid the gold escort from Forbes to Orange. The raid was carefully planned from a camp that Gardiner had set up in the mountains near Mount Wheogo and was carried out with precision and discipline, even though one of the gang, Alexander Fordyce, had fallen asleep earlier in the day under the influence of liquor and had to be raised from his stupor with dire threats. The robbers were even dressed in a kind of uniform; they all had blackened faces, wore red caps on their heads and had identical red serge shirts. Gardiner could have had no illusions about the dangers involved. He knew the coach would be heavily guarded and that the escorting police would be armed with the new rifles and six-shooters that had been issued to the recently reorganised police force. On the other hand, he knew too that, despite the routine precautions, such an attack would be unexpected as a robbery on this scale had not been attempted before.

The place chosen was just beyond a bend in the road, about 50 kilometres east of Forbes where a rocky outcrop, the Eugowra Rocks, allowed the gang to hide, out of sight of approaching traffic. One of the gang, Dan Charters, had been detailed to remain some distance away to attend the horses, which had been tethered to trees. Fences on sheep runs between the robbery site and a camp site where the men had spent the previous night had been cut to allow a clean getaway.

Some time early in the afternoon, two bullocks wagons lumbered into sight and were duly bailed up. They would provide a more effective road block than the logs Gardiner had intended to use. The wagons were placed in position in the centre of the road and the drivers forced to lie face down, as though asleep or drunk. When, soon afterwards, the escort, drawn by four horses and carrying a sergeant and three constables, rounded the bend the surprised driver was forced to swerve towards the rocky outcrop in order to negotiate the narrow passage. The bushrangers seized the moment and showered the coach and its occupants with bullets, wounding the sergeant, who was seated outside beside the driver and knocking him off the coach. One of the constables inside was also hit, but not seriously hurt, and the driver's hat was taken by a bullet. The horses reared and, as the driver tried to calm them, the four policemen exchanged a few desultory shots with the bushrangers before realising that they were outnumbered and without cover and retreated into the bush. The driver readily accepted Gardiner's shouted invitation to follow them. The wagon drivers and their loads were also speedily dispatched and the bushrangers helped themselves to the contents of the coach—almost 3000 ounces of gold, and 3000 pounds in cash, a total haul worth about 14 000 pounds.

The aftermath

The police were galvanised into action. Three days after the robbery a notice was posted in the New South Wales *Police Gazette*, offering 'One Thousand Pound Reward and Pardon to an Accomplice'—that is, 100 pounds for information leading to the conviction of each of the supposed 10 participants and a pardon to the first of the gang to turn informer.

They were spurred on in their efforts by an indignant press and the obvious delight expressed by some elements in their discomfiture. It was not long before rhyming ballads celebrating the event were written, performed and circulated. One such ballad ended with the lines:

> Gardiner—that's the Darkie is shouting loud,
> 'Hooray! Hooray, we've struck Bonanza;
> we've won the Steeplechase.
> I think we've made our fortunes at Eugowra Rocks today.'
> And so with wicked jesting the outlaws rode away.

But for most of the outlaws the 'jesting' was short-lived. Pottinger and a senior sergeant, Charles Sanderson, led parties to search the countryside around the scene of the crime. Not far from Mount Wheogo, Sanderson's party surprised a group of four horsemen who rode off at their approach, leaving behind a packhorse from which the police recovered more than one-third of the stolen gold, as well as two police rifles that had been taken from the coach by the bushrangers. Pottinger, meanwhile, had headed south on the false assumption that the miscreants would head for Victoria. On his return, however, his party happened upon John Gilbert, accompanied by his brother, Charles, and Henry Manns, one of the robbers. John Gilbert turned and sped away when Pottinger attempted to stop them, but the other two were taken into custody. Manns was found to be in possession of a quantity of gold and banknotes. As Pottinger's party approached Forbes, a gang led by Gardiner and John Gilbert attacked them and rescued the two prisoners.

Unbowed by this further humiliation, Pottinger obtained warrants and systematically searched the homes of known associates of Gardiner, including Ben Hall. Ben Hall, his brother, William, and Dan Charters were arrested by Pottinger at Hall's property; John McGuire and John Brown, Catherine's husband, were also brought in, as were Johnny O'Meally, one of the gang, and his father, Patrick. Charters soon afterwards decided to buy his freedom in return for informing on his comrades.

As it turned out, however, Charters informed only selectively, identifying only five members of the gang—Gardiner, John Gilbert, Gilbert Manns, Alexander Fordyce and John Bow—and claiming that the others—his friends O'Meally and Hall—were unknown to him and had not given names.

Fordyce, Bow and Manns were arrested and along with McGuire were charged for their involvement in the robbery. At the first trial, early in February 1863, the jury was unable to agree on a verdict. At the second, later in the month, McGuire was acquitted and the other three were found guilty and sentenced to death. There was a strong public outcry against these sentences, and a widespread feeling that it was grossly unfair for these three to pay for a crime that for which Gardiner, who remained at large, was mainly responsible. The sentences of Bow and Fordyce were later commuted, but not that of Manns. Manns had not helped his case when, in an act of misguided altruism, he added perjury to the offences he faced. In an extraordinary outburst during the second trial, he sought to exonerate Bow and Fordyce by claiming that they had not been present at the robbery.

Despite numerous petitions for clemency, Manns was hanged at Darlinghurst gaol on 26 March 1863. The hangman deliberately delayed the execution for 20 minutes, presumably in the hope that a reprieve would come. When he could wait no longer, he seemed uncharacteristically clumsy and nervous in his preparations, taking an inordinate amount of time to position the noose and pull the lever. The result was, in the words of a *Sydney Morning Herald* correspondent who was present, 'one of the most appalling spectacles ever witnessed at an execution'. The body was still convulsing after ten minutes and the hood that covered his face was spattered with blood. The body had to be lifted by four men and let fall again before Manns' agonies, and his life, were brought to an end.

Escape to Queensland

The affair between Gardiner and Catherine Brown was widely talked about, and Sir Frank Pottinger was well aware when he arrested John Brown at the end of July 1862 that he was giving Gardiner unhindered access to his lover. On the evening of Saturday 9 August, Pottinger, Sanderson and six other police hid themselves outside the Brown's slab hut near Mount Wheogo, hoping to catch Gardiner. When, some time after midnight, Gardiner rode nonchalantly into the trap that had been set, Pottinger must have thought that he had caught his man. As Gardiner passed near to where Pottinger was concealed in the bushes, the inspector took aim with his rifle, called on him to stop, and then pulled the trigger. By some mischance, the gun failed to fire, but the noise alerted Gardiner who turned and galloped off, managing to avoid the bullets fired after him by the other police.

The frustrated police then burst into the hut, and found Catherine and her young brother, John Walsh, who was asleep in bed. Cheated of his main quarry, Pottinger arrested the youngster on suspicion of being an accomplice of Gardiner's.

This was the version of the incident that Pottinger gave in his official report. Not surprisingly, other versions, even less flattering to the hapless inspector and much more titillating in their detail, were widely circulated.

Soon after this, Gardiner and Catherine contrived to leave the district together. The pair travelled by night and hid by day, and eventually found their way to a place called Apis Creek, about 100 kilometres north-west of Rockhampton. Gold had recently been discovered here and there were diggings in the area. Passing themselves off as a married couple called Christie, they were taken in by the local innkeeper and for the next 18 months helped him run the inn and local store.

Frank Gardiner's trial

They remained undetected until Catherine wrote a letter to her sister Bridget, who was now living with James Taylor in the Murrumbidgee region. Somehow, news of the letter got out—perhaps Taylor was unguarded in talking to friends in the local pub—and reached the ears of the police. In February 1864, three policemen arrived at Apis Creek disguised as miners. They befriended Gardiner, invited him to share a drink with them so that they could confirm his identity and the next morning, with the help of members of the Queensland police, had no trouble in arresting him. Gardiner was brought back to Sydney, where he arrived in mid-March.

Gardiner could not be charged with masterminding the gold escort robbery, largely because Dan Charters would not agree to testify against him. He was, instead, brought to trial in May on the charge of attempting to murder Sergeant Middleton at William Fogg's place in 1861. The prosecution, however, was careless in the presentation of its case, and Catherine had managed to procure the services of a skilled defence lawyer. Gardiner, to everyone's amazement, was acquitted.

But the authorities were determined to convict Gardiner and, if possible, to bring him to the gallows. In July 1864 he again faced court, this time on two counts, still relating to the incident at Fogg's. He was charged with the attempted murder of Middleton's offsider, William Hosie—a capital offence—and also with the lesser offence of shooting at Hosie with the intent of inflicting 'grievous bodily harm'. He was found guilty of the second offence and also of the robbery of the Wombat storekeepers, Horsington and Hewitt. Unable to pronounce a sentence of death, the judge, Chief Justice Alfred Stephen, sentenced Gardiner to a total of 32 years' hard labour.

Tragedy and then freedom

About a year later, Catherine, worn out by futile efforts to secure Gardiner's release, went to live with her sister Bridget who was now living, still with James Taylor, in the Forbes area. Despairing of ever being reunited with Gardiner, she took up with Taylor's brother, Richard, and the pair moved to the Hokitika goldfield in New Zealand. Dick Taylor proved to be a violent drunkard and the liaison was an unhappy one. Not long afterwards, Catherine committed suicide.

As the bushranging outbreaks subsided at the end of the decade, so too did the punitive zeal of the authorities. Had they known about the impending depredations of the Kelly gang, they may have been less forgiving. In 1874 Gardiner and 22 other convicted bushrangers were pardoned and freed. But while Gardiner had been shown clemency, he was not given trust. The terms of his release stipulated that he leave the Australian colonies and never return. He sailed first to Hong Kong and then to California, where he became the owner of a tavern in San Francisco.

Gardiner had been in poor health for much of his time in prison, and reportedly suffered from a heart condition. This may have been a factor in the decision to release him. However, he survived in the United States for almost another 30 years, and died of pneunomia at the venerable age of 74.

Charters, whose treachery had brought Manns to his terrible end, wisely stayed away from the Lachlan area for many years after the events described above. He was given work by the police, breaking in horses, but disappeared for some time when a Sydney newspaper reported his whereabouts—near Burwood in Sydney—and his alias, Thompson. He married in 1871 and fathered eight children. In 1873, he was arraigned in Bathurst on a charge of stealing a harness, but was acquitted. Some time early in the 1900s he moved to Grenfell, where he remained until he died, an old man of 81, in 1919.

BEN HALL
A Man of High Renown

After Frank Gardiner's retirement from the scene in the middle of 1862, his friend Ben Hall quickly emerged as the most wanted and feared bushranger in the colonies. For almost three years—until he was finally hunted down and gunned to death near Forbes early one May morning in 1865—he, in association with varying groups of accomplices, embarked upon a veritable orgy of bushranging that covered an area from Bathurst and Forbes in the north to as far south as Junee in the west and Braidwood in the east. During this extended rampage Hall and the men he led held up and robbed 10 mail coaches, 21 homesteads and stores, and stole more than 20 valuable racehorses. They also murdered two policemen.

Ben Hall was born in May 1837. In many ways the young Hall seemed an unlikely candidate for a career of crime, although he was the son of emancipist convict parents, both with a considerable record of lawbreaking. His father, Benjamin Hall, had been transported to New South Wales from England in 1825 at the age of 20 for stealing clothing. As a convict he had a history of absconding and later, when he was a free man, of cattle and horse stealing. In 1849, when Ben was 12, his father was imprisoned at Murrurundi on a number of charges of horse and cattle stealing, but was released when sufficient evidence could not be found.

His mother, Eliza, was transported from Ireland in 1829 for stealing silk. Before this she had spent a year in prison in Dublin for stealing offences and was a repeated absconder during her convict days.

Despite his brushes with the law, and several moves to different parts of the colony to avoid apprehension, Benjamin Hall senior became prosperous enough

88 Australian Bushrangers

to purchase a farm near Murrurundi, on which his son no doubt worked as a stockman. When he was about 16 the young Ben was working as a stockman in the Weddin Mountains region, south of Forbes. Three years later, in 1856, he courted and wed 16-year-old Bridget Walsh and, in 1860, in partnership with his brother-in-law, John McGuire, he took up the lease on Sandy Creek Station, near Mount Wheogo in the Lachlan district. It was a substantial property of approximately 6500 hectares on which the partners ran about 650 head of cattle.

Although he had little or no formal education, the young Ben Hall, at the age of 23, seemed destined for a reasonably prosperous future. He had not been in trouble with the law but, as John McGuire later recalled, he did indulge in cattle duffing when the opportunity arose, a practice so commonplace as to be considered less a crime than 'simply a matter of business'.

But Hall's domestic life soon turned sour. Bridget took up with a local landholder and left, taking with her their two-year-old son. It was their second child; their first had died. Hall, however, did not seem to have been a model of marital fidelity and there is some evidence that he had become involved with Ellen McGuire, his sister-in-law. Bridget's departure, according to McGuire, had nevertheless left Hall in a state of depression in which he neglected to work his property, preferring to spend his time idly firing at targets with a revolver which he had found in the bush.

Pottinger and Hall

The main catalysts in the unleashing of Hall's latent criminality were Frank Gardiner and Sir Frederick Pottinger. If the former had not come upon the scene in 1862 and the latter had not, as Hall had it, harassed him, it is likely that Hall would have regained his equanimity and settled back into a lawful existence. Given the circumstances of Hall's involvement with Gardiner, however, it is difficult to claim that Pottinger was anything but justified in his pursuit of him.

An event that could have prematurely ended Pottinger's career, and by implication have avoided the bitter enmity that developed between him and Hall, occurred in December 1861, soon after his promotion. Pottinger, whose penchant for gambling had not deserted him, was playing billiards for money in a hotel in Young when he got into an argument and physically assaulted a man, Thomas Watt, who accused him of cheating. Watt brought a charge of assault against Pottinger and the case came to court two months later. The jury found for Watt but in light of his criminal record awarded only trifling damages against Pottinger. The case came to public attention and, not for the last time, Pottinger was held up to ridicule by the press. The incident brought him a strongly worded letter of rebuke from the colonial secretary with an unambiguous warning that further such behaviour would not be tolerated.

Hall's resentment towards Pottinger reached fury pitch when, in March 1863, the inspector led a group of police to the hut Hall had built on Sandy

This photograph of Ben Hall was taken in about 1857.

Creek station and burnt it to the ground. Living in the hut at the time were Ellen McGuire and a 17-year-old girl with a young baby, which seems to have been fathered by Hall. Hall by this stage was on the run and had forfeited any rights to the property, which had been taken over by a man called Wilson. It was Wilson who had demanded that the police evict the women and then put a torch to the building. The day after burning the hut, Pottinger went back to the place and spotted Hall and another man surveying the scene. The police gave chase, but the two men got away.

By a strange irony, these two bitter enemies died within a month of each other. Pottinger died on 9 April 1865, from the effects of a gunshot wound which he had sustained about a month earlier when a pistol in his waistcoat pocket accidentally discharged.

About four months before this, in January 1865, Hall had had the satisfaction of seeing his hated rival disgraced and dismissed from the police force. In a flagrant breach of police regulations, Pottinger had ridden at a race meeting at Wowingragong, near Forbes, the same racetrack where Hall had first been arrested. To compound the irony, his horse was named Bushranger. Worse still for Pottinger, Hall and his accomplice, John Dunn, were reported to have been at the course and to have claimed that if they had wanted to, they could have 'cut him out'.

The first of the Hall gangs

The nucleus of Hall's gang in his early bushranging days consisted of two men who had taken part in and were still at large after the Eugowra Rocks hold-up—

Johnny Gilbert and John O'Meally. Another member of the gang, until he was arrested in March 1863 and sentenced to 15 years in prison, was Patrick (Patsy) Daley. Daley was only 18 when he started out with Hall and already had a reputation as a dangerous young desperado. He had been swept up in the wave of arrests that had followed the Eugowra robbery and had been charged, along with O'Meally, with rape and robbery. The charges, however, could not be made to stick.

Gilbert had been Gardiner's 'lieutenant' in his heyday. The 10-year-old Gilbert had arrived in Victoria from Canada in 1852 with his father and stepmother, who came to Australia to try their luck on the goldfields. Gilbert's mother had died while he was still an infant. By 1854, he had left his family and found work as a stable boy. He probably spent the next few years moving around the Victorian goldfields, but by 1860 was working in the Forbes area as a stockman. We do not know when he first made the acquaintance of Frank Gardiner, but by July 1861 he seems to have very much a part of his entourage when he was implicated in the rescue of Gardiner from Trooper Hosie. Gilbert was a slightly built, athletic young man of medium height, who was described in a police report in 1863 as being clean-shaven, with 'round nostrils, thick lips' and of being 'careworn in appearance'. Another police report, supposedly written by Sir Frank Pottinger, described him as having the appearance of a 'fast young squatter or stockman' and being 'particularly flash in his dress and appearance'—a description that soon earned Gilbert the sobriquet 'Flash Jack'.

After Frank Gardiner left for Queensland, Gilbert seemed to have decided to retire from bushranging. In late 1862 he left New South Wales and, with two of his brothers, Charles and James, went to New Zealand to try his luck on the goldfields there. By January 1863, however, he was back in the Forbes area and soon joined up with Hall. From then on, Gilbert proved to be the most constant of Hall's cohorts and survived his comrade by barely a week; he was shot dead during a battle with troopers near Binalong on 13 May 1865, as he and Johnny Dunn were fleeing south from the advancing police.

John O'Meally was the son of Patrick O'Meally, who had been transported for sheep stealing. In 1850, when John was 10, Patrick entered into a joint lease of a property in the Weddin Mountains with his brother-in-law, John Daley, the father of Patsy Daley. The young Patrick Daley and John O'Meally, future partners in crime, were thus thrown together very early in life. O'Meally was the same age as Gilbert, but the contrast between the two could hardly be more marked. The difference was neatly summed up by a man who was held prisoner by the Hall gang in Canowindra in October 1863. He described Gilbert as 'a very jolly fellow, of slight build and thin—always laughing'. O'Meally, he claimed was 'a murderous-looking scoundrel'.

O'Meally was a morose character whose attitude to women was predatory and violent, unlike Gilbert, who was noted for flirtatious gallantry. And it was O'Meally who, in August 1863, became the first gang member to commit murder. On a road near Cootamundra, he bailed up John Barnes, a travelling storekeeper, and shot him dead when, instead of handing over his horse as commanded, Barnes spurred it into a gallop and attempted to ride off. O'Meally met a similar end about three months later when he was shot by the owner of a station near Eugowra that the gang was ransacking.

The Hall gang, which in the early days at least was often referred to as Gilbert's gang, began their rampage in earnest from the early days of 1863. What might be called the first phase of Hall's career as a fully fledged bushranger lasted from January to June 1863. In this period, the gang of four, reduced to three after Daley's capture but with occasional other accomplices, concentrated its efforts along the road between Forbes and Young (the township at Lambing Flat had been gazetted under its new name, Young, in 1861).

Almost daily outrages occurred in this area in the next few months—the majority, but not all, of them attributable to Hall and his gang. Travellers, stations, inns and even humble settlers' huts were robbed with seeming impunity, and often with rough violence. That none of their victims, or indeed no gang members, were killed in these early days was a matter of mere good fortune.

On the evening of 2 February, for example, Hall, Gilbert, Daley, O'Meally and another accomplice bailed up a storekeeper in the settlement of Spring Creek. Daley held the storekeeper, George Dickenson, and a customer, along with two passers-by, at gunpoint in the street while the others helped themselves to cash and goods to the value of 250 pounds. Things turned dangerous when an off-duty trooper came upon the scene and attempted to disrupt the proceedings. He was seized, however, relieved of his horse and made to join the others who were being held. An attempt by the prisoners to rush Daley, who was showing signs of nervousness, further inflamed the situation. If Hall had not intervened at this point, Daley may very well have panicked and one or more of the prisoners may have been shot.

Just on four weeks later, the gang struck again, this time at a store owned by Meyers Solomon at the Big Wombat diggings. This time, shots were exchanged as Solomon had armed himself with a rifle and fired at the approaching gang. His shot missed, very narrowly, as did an answering shot from one of the gang. As the bandits were looting the store, a young employee, in a rush of heroic, if foolhardy, zeal leapt on one of the marauders and seized his pistol. Another of the gang retaliated by pointing his gun at the head of Solomon's wife and threatening to shoot her dead. The youth then surrendered the pistol, was forced to lie on the floor and was kicked savagely by Daley. Again, tragedy was narrowly averted.

The day after this, on 1 March 1863, there occurred an incident that brought the gang wide, and somewhat undeservedly admiring, publicity and that also throws light on Hall's character. Pottinger had left the district for the time being to go in search of Frank Gardiner. His place had been taken by sub-inspector John Norton. Norton and an Aboriginal tracker, William Dargin, had tracked the gang to a camp near Mount Wheogo. The bushrangers were alerted to the approach of Norton and Dargin and rode out to meet them. Norton got down and, using his horse as a shield, exchanged shots with the gang. Soon both of Norton's six-shooters were out of ammunition and he had no choice but to surrender. Hall, however, according to Norton and Dargin, then advanced on the unarmed policeman, aimed his gun at his head and pulled the trigger, intending, it seems, to kill him. He was distracted, however, by Dargin who now hurled his empty revolver at Hall before jumping back on his horse and riding away. Hall's shot narrowly missed the terrified Norton.

Hall and Daley gave chase, but Dargin managed to elude them. They then returned to where O'Meally was guarding Norton. According to Norton, Hall justified his attempted murder by saying that he had mistaken Norton for a trooper against whom he bore a grudge. The story was probably true, because the bushrangers did not molest the policeman further. Before releasing Norton, Hall took the opportunity to let his prisoner know of the strong personal resentment he felt against Pottinger for what the outlaw considered his systematic and unjust harassment. The incident served, of course, to bolster the popular myth of Hall's invulnerability and to further lower the police in popular esteem.

The authorities strike back

The morale, if not the reputation, of the police received a significant boost about a week and a half later. Pottinger, who had returned from his fruitless foray and had resumed charge of local operations, received information that the bushrangers were in the vicinity of the Pinnacle Reef diggings, which by this time had been abandoned. A party, led by Pottinger and including Dargin, tracked down Daley and gave chase. The besieged youngster took refuge in a disused mine shaft. When called upon to surrender, and on being threatened with being smoked out, he climbed out and was put under arrest. Two saddled horses stood nearby and, despite Daley's denials, Pottinger was confident that at least one other of the gang was also in the shaft. Taking his life in his hands, especially after Norton's recent close shave, Pottinger himself climbed down into the shaft to make sure it was empty.

Daley was later tried for his part in the robbery of Meyer Solomon's store. Although he had used gratuitous violence on that occasion, Daley's status as the most junior member of the gang—he was still only 19—was probably responsible for his being spared the gallows. As it turned out, he was released in 1873, after serving only two-thirds of the sentence imposed on him.

During the next three months the gang, together or in smaller groups, and sometimes with other bushrangers who joined them briefly for one of two robberies, continued their operations, extending them at times as far south as the village of Cootamundra. They supplemented the money they collected in these robberies by disposing of goods they stole from stores, homesteads and stations through a network of collaborators who were only too willing to profit from the gang's activities. In late April, for example, in company with a bushranger called Fred Lowry, Hall's gang bailed up a store in Cootamundra and made off with a huge haul of men's and women's clothes as well as tobacco and a range of saddles and other riding materials. So overloaded were they that items from their plunder were later found strewn along the road leading out of town.

Carcoar

Hall himself did not directly participate in many of the robberies carried out by his gang. In June and July 1863 O'Meally and Gilbert carried out a series of hold-ups and robberies. On 30 July, in an amazingly audacious crime which, even though it was foiled, sent shock waves through the district, and indeed the whole colony, these two held up the Commercial Banking Company in Carcoar. The incident was so unexpected, first because Carcoar, which at that time was the main commercial centre of the region, was well removed from the area in which the gang had previously operated, and second, because no bank in the colony had ever been held up before.

The two bushrangers rode into town from the direction of Blayney and hitched their horses to a rail outside the bank. As they did so they were observed by the manager of the bank, James McDonald, who was in the street at the time. McDonald saw them enter his bank and decided to follow to see what they were up to. As he came up to the door he saw Gilbert at the counter pointing a gun at the clerk. O'Meally, who was waiting near the door, attempted to force McDonald into the building. In the confusion of the moment Gilbert looked around while the clerk, seizing his opportunity, quickly grabbed a gun from beneath the counter and fired. His shot went wild but it and McDonald's shouting brought out a crowd of people who converged on the bank.

The robbers decided to cut their losses. They hurried from the bank, threatening people with their guns, and rode unmolested out of town. As if to compensate for their failure in Carcoar, they rode directly to the township of Caloola, south-east of Bathurst and relieved a local storekeeper of money and goods to the value of 300 pounds.

At about this time, two young men from the Carcoar region, John Vane and Michael (Micky) Burke, joined the gang. Both had been involved in cattle and horse stealing and, as if to prove their credentials to their new colleagues, they almost immediately pulled off a daring horse theft. In the process they committed a crime of violence that could have earned them a death sentence. Under cover of night they went to the property of Thomas Icely, a wealthy local magistrate, and stole two horses. One of them was a famous and very valuable racehorse, Comus II; the other was a grey gelding that belonged to a local police sub-inspector. As they were leaving they were surprised by the groom, an old man known as German Charley. In an exchange of fire the old man was shot in the mouth, with the bullet lodging in his throat.

This robbery, and the bank hold-up only days before, alarmed the local citizenry, almost two dozen of whom signed up as special constables to help bring the bushrangers to justice. Despite this, Hall's gang did not lack for sympathisers and collaborators. As one Carcoar resident wrote in a letter: 'I believe there is scarcely a house between Mount Macquarie and the Abercrombie River that will not afford any criminal shelter when required.' He also bemoaned the spirit of lawlessness that seemed to prevail among young men who hankered for 'the same notoriety as Gilbert and Gardiner'.

A close escape, then a murder

Carcoar could soon breathe more easily, for soon afterwards the gang turned its attentions elsewhere, at least for a while. During August 1863 the gang moved south-west and concentrated its efforts in the area from Young south to Cootamundra. On 30 August the end almost came for the outlaws when they were tracked down in the hut of a sympathiser near Wombat, just south of Young. A team of six men, including an Aboriginal tracker, took up positions outside the hut and called on the gang to surrender. Instead, they engaged the troopers in an exchange of fire, during which the leader, Senior Constable Haughey, was severely wounded in the leg—so severely that his police career was ended. Several of the police horses were also hit by bullets.

At an opportune moment the bushrangers dashed from the hut, threw themselves on their horses and rode off in different directions. In the process, however, Vane dropped his boots, which he was carrying with him as he fled. He also lost his saddle, which was not properly attached, and rode away bareback and barefoot. It was the next day, as O'Meally and Vane were holding up a cart in search of a replacement pair of boots and saddle, that the unfortunate John Barnes also happened along and was shot dead by O'Meally when he refused to stop.

Canowindra and Bathurst

This incident in no way inhibited the gang—on the very next day they robbed a store in Boorowa and their raids continued unabated throughout the next couple of months. Perhaps their most daring escapades, in which they displayed an incredible coolness and a seeming indifference to danger, involved twice taking over the township of Canowindra and once staging a raid on the major town of Bathurst.

One evening in late September Hall and his cronies ensconced themselves in Robinson's Hotel in Canowindra, having first rounded up the 40 or so townsfolk, including the local constable. They organised an all-night party at Robinson's expense, with Robinson's wife obliging by playing the piano. On the Saturday evening, 3 October, the gang of five rode openly and unrecognised down the main street of Bathurst, calmly walked into a gun store where they surveyed the merchandise and chatted to the proprietor. They then proceeded to a nearby jewellery shop. However, the proprietor's daughter recognised them and let out a series of screams that sent them scuttling from the shop. Undaunted they went to a nearby public house whose proprietor they knew had a valuable racehorse. They bailed up the proprietor, John De Clouet, all the customers in the bar and De Clouet's wife, who was bathing the children. They stole the De Clouet family's store of cash, robbed several men in the bar and then attempted to get hold of the keys to the stable to steal the racehorse, but they were foiled when the police were seen to ride past the public house. Warning their victims not to go into the street, they went to the back of the hotel where their horses were tethered and rode off. They were seen and chased by a group of troopers, but managed to outdistance them. Three days later, the gang further taunted the authorities by carrying out a series of robberies just outside Bathurst.

The second visit to Canowindra, which began in the early hours of 13 October, lasted three days and was again centred on Robinson's Hotel. Here they once again set up headquarters, bailing up visitors as they arrived, helping themselves to goods from a local store and throwing yet another lavish party. Not long after arriving, Hall went in search of the hapless local constable, only to find that he had set out to seek reinforcements. Hall rode after him, caught him up, disarmed him and brought him back to the hotel.

Crippling losses

The next few weeks produced a dramatic reversal of fortune for the Hall gang. Within a month of the second Canowindra siege, two of the five would be dead and another in custody.

The first casualty was Micky Burke, who was shot by the assistant gold commissioner, Henry Keightley, when the gang was besieging his homestead at Dunn's Plains, near Rockley. Keightley, knowing that such an attack was possible, had a loaded gun ready, and on seeing the bushrangers approach he quickly retreated into his house and took up a position behind the door from where he exchanged fire with his attackers. He managed to get Burke in his sights and fired, hitting the young man in the abdomen. Burke did not die from this shot, but was in such agony that he shot himself in the head. Even then he did not die immediately.

In the house with Keightley were his wife, Caroline, the Keightley's baby, a servant and a visitor, Dr Pechey. Keightley's gun was soon out of ammunition and, as he was unable to reach his store of extra guns and ammunition without exposing himself to the bushrangers' fire, those inside had no choice but to surrender. A scene of great confusion followed as an hysterical Vane threatened to shoot Keightley to avenge his mate's death, and the servant and Dr Pechey intervened on his behalf. Pechey then observed that Burke was not dead and offered to treat him if he was allowed to ride into Rockley to collect his instruments. He was permitted to go after giving an undertaking not to report the incident. While he was gone, however, Burke did die, which led to a further outburst of grief by Vane and renewed threats to kill Keightley.

Hall then resolved the impasse by proposing what must at first have seemed a preposterous solution. For shooting Burke, Keightley would have earned himself a reward of 500 pounds. Hall offered to spare Keightley for a payment of that sum. The offer was accepted, but 500 pounds was not to be found on the premises. Caroline Keightley was then told that she and Dr Pechey could ride to her father's property just out of Bathurst, a distance of more than 60 kilometres, to try to obtain the money. A deadline the following afternoon was set for her return. Caroline Keightley duly returned the next morning with the money, Keightley was released and the intruders departed.

As a result of this incident, the reward for the capture, dead or alive, of any of the four members of the Hall gang was increased to 1000 pounds.

Almost immediately after the death of Burke, Vane decided to leave the gang. He sought advice from a Father Timothy McCarthy, the Catholic parish priest of Carcoar. McCarthy advised him to surrender to the authorities. On

This 1894 painting, by Patrick William Maroney, depicts the death of John O'Meally during the raid on Goimbla Station in November 1863.

19 November 1863 Vane and McCarthy went to the courthouse in Bathurst, where Vane formally surrendered and was taken into custody. When brought to trial he was sentenced to life imprisonment.

On the evening of the day that Vane surrendered, O'Meally met his death. It was during a raid on David Campbell's Goimbla Station near Eugowra, carried out by Hall, Gilbert and O'Meally. Like Keightley, Campbell immediately seized a rifle when he heard suspicious noises on the verandah of his house at about nine o'clock. His suspicions were confirmed when a man opened fire through an open doorway. Campbell returned the fire and the bushranger retreated to join his mates, who then laid siege to the house, threatening to burn it down if the occupants did not come out. To reinforce their point, the gang then set fire to Campbell's barn.

As the barn burned, Campbell caught sight of O'Meally silhouetted against the flames and, taking careful aim, shot him through the head. After that Gilbert and Hall must have hastily quit the scene because when, several hours later, Campbell went carefully outside to investigate, all he found were a cabbage-tree hat and a rifle. The next morning O'Meally's body was found near some trees where Hall and Gilbert had dragged it. His pockets were empty and a mark on one of his fingers clearly indicated that a ring had recently been removed from it.

New accomplices

Undeterred by the loss of their mate, Hall and Gilbert continued to rob and plunder. Just a week after the Goimbla fiasco they held up the Burrowa mail coach, and in the next month they robbed coaches travelling between Wellington and Orange, and Wagga Wagga and Yass.

It was not long before two new faces joined the gang. They were a strangely contrasting pair. James Gordon, also known as Mount, was in his late 50s and was often referred to as 'the old man'. He had come to New South Wales from Ireland in 1850 as a free settler, but seven years later had been convicted of robbery and had served a term on a road gang. He was freed in 1861. James Dunleavy was a 17-year-old lad from Forbes.

Gilbert seems to have left the gang sometime in August 1864 and gone to Victoria. Rumours abounded throughout the colony about the reasons for his disappearance. One report stated that, sick of the bushranging life, he had managed to steal away on a ship to the United States. Another claimed he and Hall had quarrelled over a woman and had fired shots at each other. Whatever the truth, Gilbert was not away for long, for by October he was back and had brought with him a new recruit: a hot-headed 17-year-old ex-groom and jockey, John Dunn, who was wanted by the police for absconding from bail on a recent robbery charge. The lad came, then, with excellent credentials.

A gang of three

The 'new' gang, however, numbered only three, for during Gilbert's absence both Gordon and Dunleavy had followed Vane's example and surrendered to the authorities. Dunleavy was the first to leave. In August he had been badly wounded in the wrist during a shoot-out with police near Bogolong. Hall had also been wounded, but less seriously, in the arm. Dunleavy suffered considerable pain from this wound, which refused to heal. Late in September Dunleavy left the gang and made contact with another Catholic priest, took his advice and surrendered in Bathurst. He was sentenced to 15 years.

Gordon's disillusionment came in early October. He simply packed up and rode out of the camp and was captured soon afterwards by troopers. He was sentenced to 25 years.

Now left alone, Hall may have contemplated surrender. According to Father Timothy McCarthy, who had earlier persuaded Vane to give himself up, Hall had had discussions with him and had even undertaken to surrender 'within a month'. McCarthy, it seems, had all kinds of contacts who came to him with information which led him to the bushrangers—contacts who would have been unwilling to pass on similar information to the police. Probably unbeknown to Hall, McCarthy was also talking to no less a personage than the inspector general of police for New South Wales, who encouraged him in his efforts to 'save' Hall.

Thoughts of surrender, if indeed Hall ever seriously entertained them, were abandoned with the return of Gilbert and his promising young protégé. Soon afterwards, any such thoughts would have been rendered futile as the result of the death of a policeman in one of the gang's operations, which by this time had moved further south to the area between Wagga Wagga and Yass. It happened on 17 November 1864 when the gang attempted to hold up the mail coach travelling from Gundagai to Jugiong. They had in fact held up this coach only two days earlier, and four days before that they had robbed the Yass mail coach. The mails in this area were clearly unsafe and a decree was issued that the mail coaches were to be accompanied by armed troopers.

When, then, the mail coach approached the point where the bushrangers were waiting for it, there was one armed guard sitting beside the driver and two others riding behind. Hall and Gilbert rode straight towards the two mounted troopers and engaged them in a shoot-out. Gilbert's adversary was a Sergeant Parry and the duel between them ended in Parry's being shot in the head and chest and falling dead off his horse. The other mounted trooper surrendered to Hall and Dunn when he hit his head on the branch of a tree.

The death of Sergeant Parry, as shown in the
Illustrated Sydney News *of 30 May 1874.*

The third guard had raised his gun to shoot at the bushrangers but had been ordered by a magistrate who was travelling in the coach not to do so, in case it attracted the bushrangers' fire in his direction. Under orders not to shoot, the unfortunate constable took off into the bush.

Observing this ugly scene was quite a crowd of people, including a mounted trooper, James McLaughlin, that the bushrangers had earlier disarmed. The others were the passengers and drivers of a number of carts and wagons that the bandits had robbed earlier that day as they waited for the main prize. Gilbert announced to the horrified onlookers that the 'bloody fool' lying dead before them was the first man he had ever shot, adding that 'I don't like to shoot a man'.

The three men were now branded as murderers and warrants were issued for their arrest on that charge. If captured there was now no chance of receiving a sentence less than death.

Just over two months later, Dunn was responsible for the murder of another policeman. Early in the evening of 26 January 1865, Hall, Gilbert and Dunn held up the Commercial Hotel at the township of Collector. The proprietor and several customers were forced outside, where Dunn was left to guard them. As a rider approached the inn, Dunn fired at him, and he turned and rode away. The gunfire alerted the local constable, Samuel Nelson, who was alone on duty at the time. He set out to investigate, accompanied by his 17-year-old son, Frederick. As Nelson walked towards the inn, he ignored Dunn's call to stop and strode doggedly onwards, only to receive a mortal wound to the stomach. As he fell he dropped his rifle, Dunn then stepped up to the writhing figure and shot him at point-blank range in the face.

The net begins to tighten

About this time the gang began to suffer a series of reverses as the police efforts intensified. Whatever public sympathy they may have enjoyed began to wane and people became more inclined to confront rather than comply with the demands of the bandits.

About a week and a half after the murder of Nelson, the gang was bettered by four young sons of a squatter, W P Faithfull of Springfield Station, south of Goulburn. A wagon, driven by Percy, the eldest Faithfull boy, came out of the gates of Springfield Station and was called upon to stop. Instead of complying, one of the boys fired a rifle and another began firing with a revolver. Shots continued to be fired on both sides, one of which hit Gilbert's horse in the head, killing it and bringing Gilbert crashing to the ground. Another shot crashed into a fence behind which Gilbert had quickly taken cover. As the wagon, which had been turned around, neared the gates, the boys leapt out and, pursued by Hall, raced for the homestead. Fearing that they would be able to fire on him from the cover of the house, Hall retreated and the gang, with Gilbert sharing Dunn's horse, retired from the scene. It was a humiliating defeat.

Another spectacular defeat occurred on 13 March when the gang, this time in company with Thomas Clarke, who with his brother John would later form a formidable bushranging pair, attempted to rob the Araluen gold escort. They took up a position where the escort, which contained 54 000 ounces of gold, would have to labour up a steep incline. As the escort approached, a shot rang out and one of four troopers, Constable Kelly, fell to the ground, severely wounded. He managed to drag himself behind a dirt bank from where he could fire at the bushrangers with his revolver. Another trooper took cover behind the wheel of the cart and the other two wheeled around to take up a position behind the four assailants. Seeing that they would be surrounded, the gang beat a strategic retreat.

The net tightened further when the *Felons Apprehension Act (1865)* was proclaimed. This put further pressure on the bushrangers and their supporters as it stipulated harsh penalties for anyone convicted of harbouring them and gave the police powers to acquire horses, food and other goods from citizens in their search for the bushrangers. As well, on 17 April, a summons was issued ordering Hall, Gilbert and Dunn to surrender by 29 April or else be declared outlaws. This would mean that they could be shot on sight, and without warning, by anybody who saw them.

The end

It appears, despite a continuation of the gang's activities, that Hall, Gilbert and Dunn decided at this stage to split up. Hall stayed on alone at a bush camp near Goobang Creek, about 30 kilometres out of Forbes, while Gilbert and Dunn travelled south, perhaps making for Victoria.

On the evening of 4 May a party of six police and two Aboriginal trackers, one of whom was William Dargin, came upon Hall's camp. In charge was

This sketch, which appeared in the Illustrated Melbourne Post *of 25 May 1865, gives a highly melodramatic depiction of Hall's death.*

Sub-inspector James Davidson, who had taken over Pottinger's duties after he had been forced to resign. Their success in finding Hall was due partly to information supplied by former collaborators of the bushranger, but also largely to Dargin's well-honed tracking skills.

The first sign they saw of the camp was two horses, hobbled in the scrub. They watched these until about ten o'clock in the evening when a man they assumed to be Hall came along, led the horses to another spot and then went back into the scrub. The party then settled for a night of watching in the freezing cold. Early the next morning Hall emerged again into the open, and Davidson, Dargin and another policeman ran towards him. As Hall turned to flee, all three fired and Hall ran to a sapling and held on to it. At this stage the police party went berserk. Davidson admitted in a report that he lost control over his men, who were 'perfectly mad'. A total of about 15 shots were fired into the inert body of the dead bushranger. The body, thus riddled, was draped over a horse and taken to Forbes, where it was placed on public display.

Three days later, Gilbert and Dunn were seen near Carcoar. Both the men and their horses were described as looking close to exhaustion. On 13 May they were tracked to a house near Binalong. The police rushed the house, but Gilbert and Dunn escaped through a back window. Giving pursuit, Gilbert ran into a nearby creek bed where a well-aimed shot ended his life. Dunn, although wounded in the leg, managed to outrun his pursuers and escaped.

Dunn remained at large for another seven months. He was finally tracked down in late December 1865 hiding out in the remote Macquarie Marshes. In the ensuing chase, Dunn was seriously wounded in the back and one of the policemen was shot in the groin. He was tried and found guilty in Sydney in February 1866 and sentenced to death by Chief Justice Sir Alfred Stephen. He was hanged at Darlinghurst gaol in March 1866. At his execution he was attended by the Catholic prison chaplain and Father Timothy McCarthy, the priest who had earlier offered counsel to both John Vane and Ben Hall.

'MAD DAN' MORGAN
A Cold-blooded Killer

A month before Ben Hall's bullet-torn body was paraded through the streets of Forbes and then placed on public display to satisfy the collective morbid curiosity of the townsfolk, the body of another bushranger suffered an even more extreme desecration in the northern Victorian town of Wangaratta. The man who called himself Dan Morgan, but who was universally referred to as 'Mad Dan' Morgan, had rivalled Hall's notoriety during the previous two years and his name had inspired considerably greater dread.

Because Hall and Dan Morgan were operating simultaneously in New South Wales, it was sometimes assumed that they were in league. However, while Morgan may well have been inspired to an outlaw's career by the much-publicised doings of Gardiner and Hall, it is highly unlikely that Hall and Morgan ever met, let alone worked together. For one thing they operated in different territories; Morgan's attacks occurred in the Riverina district between the Murrumbidgee and Murray rivers, while Hall's took place mainly around the Lachlan. For another, they would almost certainly have proved incompatible. The contrasts between them, both physical and behavioural, were extremely marked. Morgan was unprepossessing, and even threatening, in appearance. His aquiline nose gave him a distinctly predatory look, an impression that was reinforced by his wild, black bushy beard and unkempt hair. He was essentially a loner, brooding and vengeful, with a gruff, uncivil manner. His violent swings of mood and irrational violence were what earned him the sobriquet Mad Dan. Hall, on the other hand, was handsome, gregarious and capable of great charm and civility. While he did not eschew violence, he tended to use it judiciously and hardly ever gratuitously. What the two had in common was their superb assurance on horseback and a certain ungainliness on foot. Hall limped as a result of a childhood accident; Morgan was known to be awkward and slow on his legs.

Early days

Morgan's early history is obscure and there are varying reports of his origins and upbringing. However, it is generally thought that he was born near Campbelltown in New South Wales some time about 1830, the son of a convict, George Fuller, and a prostitute, Mary Owen. He seems to have been adopted early on by John Roberts, a hawker who operated near Appin and who was known locally as 'Jack the Welshman'. The young boy's education was haphazard or nonexistent, and he is reported to have developed his solitary habits early by living for long periods in the bush. He was later renowned for his marksmanship, a skill he no doubt developed in these early experiences foraging in the bush. Like many bushrangers before him he became a proficient horse stealer and rider when very young. According to one tradition, he spent six months in Berrima gaol during the late 1840s for having assaulted a policeman.

In the early 1850s he followed the gold-seeking crowds that flocked to Victoria, but did not seem to look for gold himself. Instead, he went to the area near Avoca where he lived in a succession of simple bark structures, similar to the 'gunyahs' that Aboriginal people used as temporary shelters, indulging in horse stealing and other acts of theft and eking out an existence from the fruits of the bush. At this stage he was known in the area as 'Native Bill'.

In April 1854 he came to more conspicuous public notice when he held up and robbed a hawker name John Duff near the Castlemaine diggings. He was tracked down and arrested about three weeks later and brought back to Castlemaine. On the way he attempted an impossible escape and was badly wounded as a result of being struck on the head with a policeman's revolver and dragged along the ground by the frightened horse to which he was handcuffed. In June 1854, when his injuries had healed sufficiently, he was brought to trial under the name of John Smith before Mr Justice, later Sir, Redmond Barry, the judge who would later sentence Ned Kelly to death. He was found guilty and sentenced to 12 years' prison with hard labour.

Dan Morgan

In 1860 he was released on a ticket-of-leave and sent to the area around Yackandandah in north-eastern Victoria, where he was required to report regularly to the police. This he failed to do and from here on he was officially listed as being illegally at large. He immediately returned to his previous driftless, predatory lifestyle. Not long after, he was slightly wounded in an incident over which he brooded for the next five years and which he harboured an unrelenting yearning to avenge. He had been pursued into the bush after he stole a horse from a remote station at Whitfield on the King River. The station owner, Thomas Evans, and his sons, accompanied by another squatter, Edmond Bond, gave chase and one of the Evans sons, Evan, emptied a barrel load of buckshot into the thief's right arm and shoulder. Morgan escaped, nursing his wound and his smouldering resentment.

Back in New South Wales

There is no record of Morgan from this point until about the middle of 1863, when, now calling himself Daniel Morgan, after a pirate of that name, he was robbing homesteads, stations and travellers in the area around Wagga Wagga. At this stage he was in league with an accomplice, known only as 'German Bill'. One day in August, Morgan and his partner bailed up a stranger who was travelling alone on horseback between Wagga Wagga and Urana. Instead of doing the brigands' bidding, however, the man raced off along the road, only to be overtaken and forced to stop by the bushrangers on their superior mounts. He turned out to be Henry Bayliss, the police magistrate at Wagga Wagga. According to Bayliss's later account of the meeting, Morgan tried to extract from him a promise not to report the encounter, a promise Bayliss

Map of New South Wales and Victoria showing: Urangeline, Doodal Cooma Swamp, Henty, Culcairn, Walla Walla, Round Hill homestead, Yarrawonga, Tumbarumba, Peechelba, Albury, Wangaratta, Morgan shot here, Castlemaine, Melbourne.

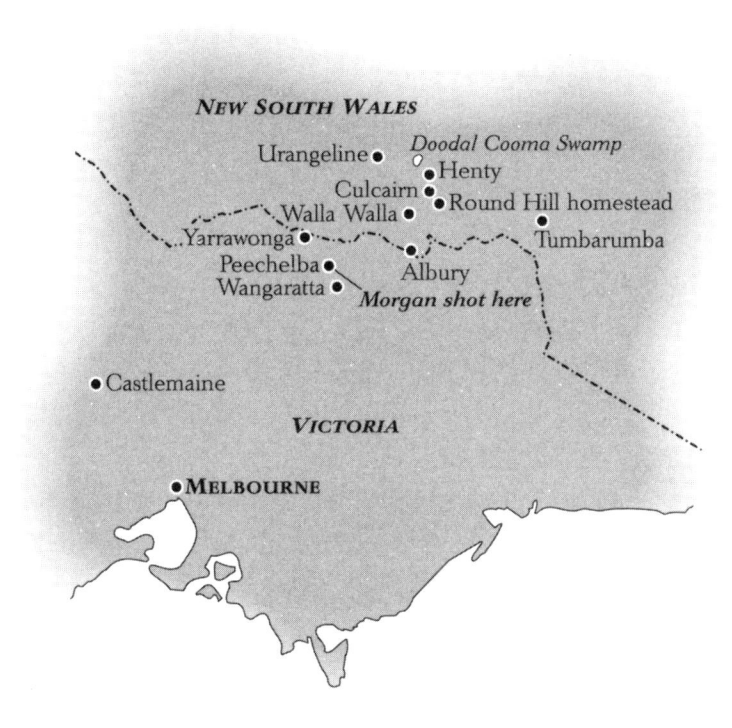

refused to make. If the account is true, Bayliss, given Morgan's later record, was lucky to survive the incident. Instead, Morgan sent Bayliss on his way after relieving him of what money he had on him. As soon as he arrived at Urana, where he was to hold court, Bayliss immediately telegraphed the information about Morgan's whereabouts to the Wagga Wagga police, who began to organise a search party.

The party, which comprised three policemen plus Bayliss as a guide, set out some days late and made for the region where Bayliss had encountered Morgan. They found a simple bark hut with the embers of a fire outside, which they assumed was Morgan's. They staked out an ambush, but as night fell were forced inside by the onset of heavy rain. When he heard a noise, Bayliss left the hut only to be fired on by German Bill. The shot missed, but in a further exchange both shots found their marks. Bayliss's shot severely wounded his adversary, who died later as a result. German Bill's shot also inflicted a severe, but not fatal, wound. The bullet hit Bayliss on the right thumb, then travelled up his arm and came out at the back near the shoulder blade. Bayliss, even in his desperate condition, was preparing to fire again when Morgan appeared at very close quarters and fired at his head, missing narrowly but singeing his face and causing him to lose consciousness.

The encounter must have unleashed some malevolent force in Morgan who for the next sixteen and a half months went on a murderous rampage that earned him the title the 'terror of the Riverina'.

A cycle of violence

The Bayliss incident resulted in a price of 200 pounds being placed on Morgan's head. But many who might have informed on the bushranger were deterred, at least for the moment, by fear of reprisal. It seems likely that many of Morgan's robberies went unreported because of the terror he inspired in pastoralists. In December 1864 a Deniliquin newspaper bitterly accused a local station holder of 'holding a candle to the devil' by directing his employees to comply with any demands Morgan might make and even leave food and other supplies out for him in the event that he might call.

Within days of the Bayliss episode, a shepherd on a nearby station was shot dead. The crime was generally assumed, perhaps wrongly, to be Morgan's revenge for the shepherd's role as an informer. He was certainly merciless with those he considered his enemies.

In November 1863, for example, he turned up at Mittagong Station because he believed that the manager, Isaac Vincent, had informed against him. He forced some of the farm labourers to tie Vincent to a fence adjacent to the woolshed and then to set fire to the shed and its contents. He gave every indication to the terrified manager, his distraught mother and horrified onlookers that he would allow Vincent to be consumed by the spreading flames until at the last minute he cut him loose. Before leaving, Morgan forced the shearers to burn down the station's store. Guilty or not of being an informer, Vincent paid a huge price—the losses were estimated at about 3000 pounds—for the suspicions he had aroused.

The attack on Mittagong Station was clearly premeditated. Even more ominous, however, was the fear of Morgan's sudden and seemingly unprovoked murderous rages, or the summary or spontaneous revenge he meted out several times. The most notorious example of such a rage and such summary revenge

Morgan goes berserk at Round Hill Station, near Culcairn, in June 1864.

occurred at Round Hill Station, near Culcairn, on Sunday 19 June 1864. Four men—Samuel Watson, the station manager; John McLean, the cattle overseer; John Heriot, a neighbouring squatter's son; and a cattle dealer named McNeil—were talking in a room of the homestead when Morgan and two accomplices rode up. Morgan strode up onto the verandah and bailed up the four men. He had them gather up the stationhands, take them outside near a shed and serve them rounds of grog. The two anonymous accomplices watched from a distance.

This was not the first time Morgan had ostentatiously cast himself in the role of defender and benefactor of the underdog. Only a short time before he had raided the nearby Walla Walla Station and conspicuously enquired about the working conditions of the stationhands, adding that he wanted to be informed if they were badly treated at any time. Like other bushrangers, Morgan was keenly aware of the 'public relations' value of such an exercise.

On this occasion something of a festive atmosphere seemed to be developing until Watson made a chance remark about the provenance of the stirrups on Morgan's horse. Morgan suddenly went berserk and started firing wildly in the direction of the assembled group, who promptly abandoned their liquor and dispersed for whatever cover they could find. Young Heriot was hit in the leg and a shot aimed directly at Watson's head passed through his hand that was put up in defence and grazed the side of his skull. Morgan raged around the yard, threatening and firing, until, seeing Heriot dragging himself painfully across the ground, he placed a revolver against his head, making as if to shoot him dead. Watson then bravely intervened on Heriot's behalf and Morgan suddenly relented, substituting solicitous care for his former demented fury and calling on all and sundry to come to the aid of the wounded men. He apologised to Watson and blamed the effects of drink for his erratic behaviour.

He supervised some rudimentary attention to Heriot's leg and Watson's hand and agreed that McLean be allowed to ride to Walla Walla to seek qualified medical help. However, McLean had hardly left when Morgan, suddenly suspicious, stormed out the house, mounted his horse and set off at furious speed. He caught up with McLean and unceremoniously shot him in the back. Once again, his mood swung back. He picked up the critically hurt McLean, propped him on his horse and shepherded him back to the station, where he remained, exuding sympathy, for several hours before riding off with his accomplices. McLean died two days later, but not before—at least according to the evidence given at the official inquest by a stockman—Morgan had returned to the station and had sat contritely beside the dying man's bedside for some time. If this did occur, it is perhaps as much an indication of Morgan's deranged state of mind and lack of sound judgment as were his violent outbursts—the countryside all around was being combed by search parties.

Police killings

Despite any such feelings of contrition, Morgan's vengefully murderous mood remained with him. A mere five days later he committed what seems to have been another spontaneous killing. Exactly what happened is uncertain because the only firsthand account of the event is a possibly self-justifying one given by a trooper whose behaviour was later judged to be cowardly. As Sergeant David Maginnerty and Trooper Churchley were patrolling the road between Culcairn and Tumbarumba they came upon Morgan riding ahead of them in the same direction. Maginnerty spurred his horse onwards to check on who it was and, as he drew near, Morgan drew his gun, turned in the saddle and shot the policeman in the chest.

Morgan's cold-blooded murder of Sergeant Maginnerty, as portrayed in the Illustrated Sydney News *of 17 August 1864.*

According to Churchley's account the shot caused his horse to rear up, allowing Morgan to make a getaway. He claims to have pursued Morgan and exchanged fire with him once he had regained control of his horse. Such a claim seems questionable in the light of the fact that when the body was recovered the next day, it had been searched and some possessions removed, presumably by Morgan. In the wake of this murder, the reward for the capture of Morgan was increased from 500 to 1000 pounds. One hundred pounds was also offered for information about people harbouring or helping the outlaw.

Morgan's very early experience of existing alone in the bush stood him in good stead for the kind of life he was now living and gave him a decided advantage over the numerous search parties that were sent out in pursuit of him. The countryside he now inhabited was rugged, heavily timbered and mountainous. Morgan's finely honed bush survival and hunting skills allowed him the 'luxury' of remaining for long periods in inaccessible regions without the need to venture into settled areas in search of sustenance. Indeed, it seems that much of Morgan's marauding was motivated more by revenge and an innate desire to create havoc than by any physical needs. In the last three months of 1864 Morgan staged only three attacks, one of them on a station and the other two on mail coaches. For the rest of the time he remained hidden in the forests.

The reason for this relative inactivity may well have been the public outrage created by an atrocity he perpetrated against a police search party on the night of 4 September 1864. A group of four police, led by Senior Sergeant Thomas Smyth, was settling down for the night at their campsite at a place called Doodal Cooma Swamp, near Henty. They were unaware of the proximity of their quarry until a volley of bullets tore through the canvas of their tent, wounding Smyth in the chest. The other three troopers exchanged fire with Morgan, who seems to have had at least one accomplice with him, but he made good his escape. Smyth was taken to Albury, where he died three and a half weeks later.

New outburst and a closing net

Morgan burst back on the scene spectacularly in mid-January 1865. Near Kyeamba, about halfway between Wagga Wagga and Tumbarumba, he first held up a road contractors' camp, then robbed a group of five Chinese. When the surprised and uncomprehending Chinese misunderstood his intentions, he shot one of them in the arm. Taking some of the road workers with him, he travelled across country to a place called Little Billabong where he robbed two more travellers. He then ordered the road workers to cut the telegraph line linking Albury to Sydney before holding up and robbing the Albury mail coach. Allowing his prisoners to go free, he finished perhaps the busiest day of his criminal career by bailing up two hawkers who were unwisely travelling the road after dark.

Robberies and raids, and at least one revenge-motivated shooting, continued during February and March. On 2 April 1864, Morgan crossed the Murray River into Victoria. He had already given notice of his intentions by bragging during a robbery at Jerilderie that the Victorian police would be just as frightened as the New South Wales police 'to go near any place where they thought they might find him'. When this was reported in a local newspaper, the editorial writer predicted that Morgan would last no longer that 48 hours in the southern colony.

In fact, Morgan lasted just six days. His vengeful instincts took him south towards Whitfield Station where, five years earlier, young Evan Evans had wounded him in the arm. After stealing a racehorse and robbing a station on the way, he arrived at Whitfield before first light on 6 April and set fire to the haystacks. He demanded that the surprised and still sleepy stationhands produce

Evan Evans and, when they could not because he was away from the property, he forced his brother John Evans to stand between two burning haystacks. Fortunately for everyone, his fury diminished and he left without causing any further damage.

There are some curiously prophetic parallels between the ending of the Dan Morgan story and that of the last and most celebrated of Australian bushrangers, Ned Kelly. The circumstances of Morgan's last night on earth were uncannily similar to those of Kelly's last stand at the nearby Glenrowan Hotel.

As he made his way north again towards New South Wales, Morgan stopped at a dairy near Glenrowan, claiming that he was on his way to rob the Glenrowan Inn. A police party of four, led by Superintendent Winch from Beechworth and Detective Manwaring, who had been directing the hunt for Morgan in New South Wales, were now in pursuit. When they were told of Morgan's stated intention, they immediately, and correctly, assumed it was a ruse. Instead, they set up an ambush along the main road north from Melbourne.

Morgan whiles away the evening, enjoying Mrs McPherson's music, before his death at Peechelba Station.

Morgan, however, had cut across country and late in the afternoon of 8 April happened upon Robert Telford, the overseer of nearby Peechelba Station. He forced Telford at gunpoint to take him to the station homestead. There were two homesteads on this extensive sheep station, one belonging to Ewen McPherson and the other, about half a kilometre away, to the joint owner of the property, George Rutherford. Telford took Morgan to the McPherson house, which was set back in the bush and out of sight of Rutherford's homestead.

Morgan commandeered the surprised household, gathering the family and stationhands from the adjacent buildings together. He demanded and was given a meal, and then became expansively conversational as he reminisced about his exploits. In this uncharacteristically mellow frame of mind, he sat gun in hand by the piano as two of the young women of the household provided him with musical entertainment. Lulled by this tranquil domestic scene and by the

Morgan is shot and mortally wounded at Peechelba Station, near Wangaratta, Victoria.

'Mad Dan' Morgan 117

Morgan's body, grotesquely posed for a photograph.

whisky he was consuming—and unaware that there was another household close by—Morgan allowed one of the female servants to leave the house on the pretext of needing to see to a sick child.

The young woman managed to get word to Rutherford, who promptly sent one of his men on a late night ride to Wangaratta to alert the police. The next morning the trap was set.

Morgan was ambushed while attempting to leave the station. Members of the posse of police and stationhands that had surrounded the homestead had been instructed to shoot at his legs so that he could be taken alive, but when Morgan emerged from the house, accompanied by the station owner and members of his household on the morning of 9 April 1865, an impulsive young stationhand fired prematurely, mortally wounding him in the neck. Morgan died in the station's woolshed about five hours later. His body was then removed to Wangaratta where it was sat up in a grotesquely life-like pose, complete with pistol in hand and eyes staring blankly past propped up eyelids, for the benefit of a photographer. It was then gruesomely mutilated. His long black beard was first unceremoniously ripped off, along with a patch of skin, by a souvenir-hungry police superintendent, and then, on the order of the coroner, his head was severed and sent to Melbourne in the interests of phrenological research.

Superintendent Cobham and the coroner, Dr Dobbyn, were later severely reprimanded for their actions, but they were not removed from their positions. Cobham's claim that his act of barbarity was justified because Morgan was considered to be 'outside the pale of civilisation' was dismissed as unacceptable.

Yet Cobham's assertion was true to some extent, because Morgan, at least in New South Wales, had been placed officially beyond the pale of civilisation. Like Ben Hall, he had, at the time of his death, been about to be declared an outlaw under the recently proclaimed Felons Apprehension Act. Under the provisions of this act anyone, whether in the police or not, would have been entitled to shoot him on sight, and without warning.

THOMAS AND JOHN CLARKE

Brothers-in-arms

There was something distinctly unglamorous, even anticlimactic, about the capture of the Clarke brothers in 1867. Not only did their outlawing career end in a rather inglorious surrender, but they also, at least according to one observer, failed to fit the image that the publicity surrounding their exploits had created. When Thomas and John Clarke were brought to Sydney by ship to stand trial, a large crowd gathered at the wharf to see them disembark. Fed on stories of brutal murder and mayhem, these curious observers, no doubt expecting to see signs of overt malevolence or at least a bearing of arrogant disdain, were disconcerted to be presented with 'two sheepish-looking, overgrown youths' rather than the 'ferocious, bloodthirsty' characters of popular repute.

One day in September 1866 four strangers arrived in the area around the town of Braidwood in south-eastern New South Wales. They set up camp in the rugged, mountainous country to the south-west of Braidwood on the eastern slopes of the Great Dividing Range and passed themselves off to the local inhabitants as surveyors. Most of the locals were small landholders and farmers, although since gold was discovered at nearby Araluen in 1852 and then later at Major's Creek and other locations in the vicinity, the area was also home to thousands of gold prospectors. Braidwood owed its size and importance to the gold discoveries and it was the administrative capital of the region. It was also the centre of a thriving pastoral industry dominated by a number of wealthy station owners with large landholdings.

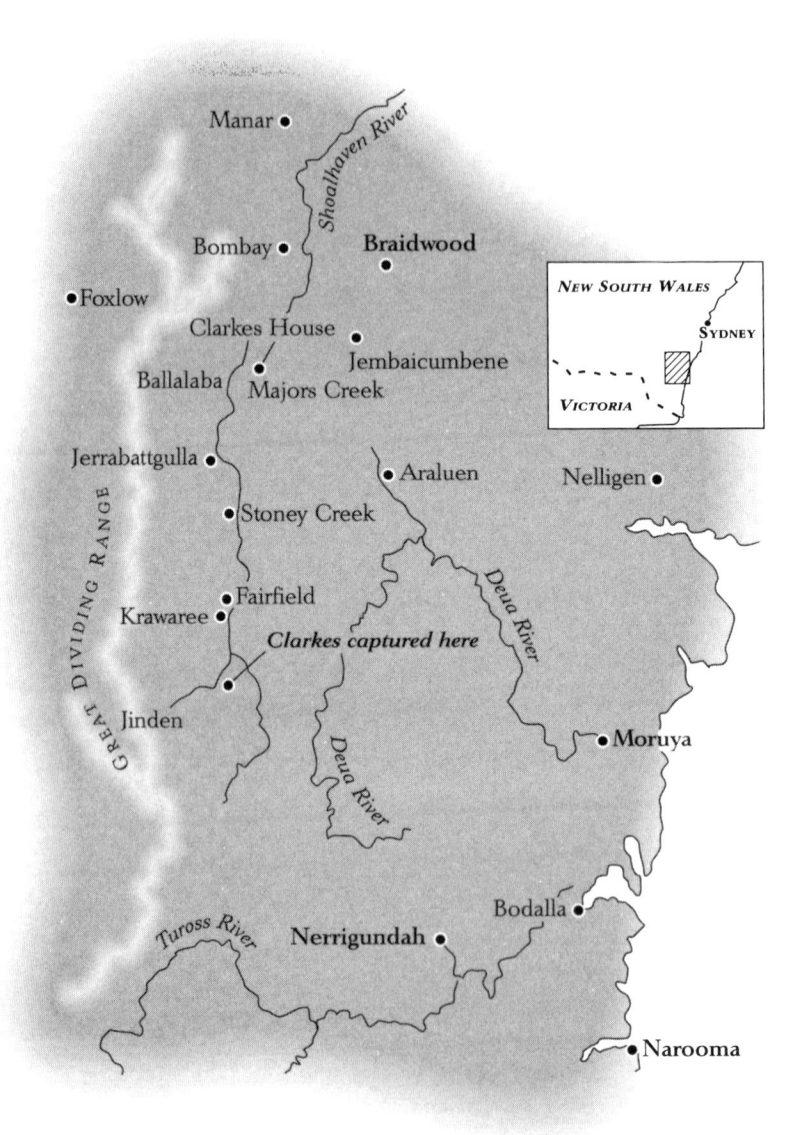

The combination of gold, pastoral wealth and a rugged terrain that was difficult of access acted as a magnet to all kinds of law-breakers—cattle duffers, horse stealers, petty thieves and, more seriously, bushrangers and highway robbers. And it was bushrangers that the four strangers had really come to 'survey'. Specifically they were there to hunt down a murderous gang which had been operating in the area for the previous two years. This gang was led by Thomas

Clarke and included in its changing composition his younger brother, John, his uncles, Patrick Connell and Thomas Connell (they were his mother's brothers, but were considerably younger than their sister), Bill and Joe Berryman, and Bill Scott, whom a local policeman had described as someone who would 'deliberately shoot any man in New South Wales for sixpence'. Two months earlier, in April 1866, Thomas Clarke had murdered a policeman during a daring raid on the settlement of Nerrigundah, the centre of the goldmining area known as the 'Gulph' diggings.

In what was by now a well-established tradition, the gang had bailed up a number of people they had robbed along the way, one of whom they had shot in the thigh for refusing to co-operate, in a nearby hotel. Then, leaving their prisoners there under guard, they had ridden into Nerrigundah, commandeered one of the hotels there and then gone to rob the local gold dealer. It was while they were in the store that the two local policeman came on the scene. One of them, Constable O'Grady, had been roused from his bed where he was ill with a fever. In the ensuing exchange of fire, one of the gang members, a young jockey and gold fossicker called William Fletcher, who had never previously fallen foul of the law, was shot dead. By now it was dark, and Thomas Clarke, catching sight of O'Grady in the light of a window, ran after him and shot him down.

As a result of this Thomas Clarke was declared an outlaw under the *Felons Apprehension Act (1865)* and a reward of 500 pounds was placed on his head. As well, a number of volunteer police parties were organised to help local police in their efforts to capture the gang. Four volunteers were recruited from among the warders at Darlinghurst gaol in Sydney and it was these who, led by John Carroll, went to the Braidwood area under the guise of surveyors. One of the four, John Phegan, had previously worked in the area and had a good knowledge of the terrain.

Criminal pedigree

Thomas Clarke and his two brothers, John and James, could boast impeccable criminal credentials and connections. Their father, John Clarke, had been transported from County Down in Ireland for pig stealing and on being released had settled in the Braidwood area, where he had married Mary Connell, the daughter of free immigrants from County Limerick. Two of Mary's four brothers

122   Australian Bushrangers

were involved with Thomas and John's exploits and the other two were also involved in serious clashes with the law.

John and Mary Clarke had five children: Thomas, James and John, and two daughters, Anne and Margaret. Both Anne and Margaret were generally supposed to consort with bushrangers. In April 1867, Anne, who was about 20 at the time, had been reported in a local newspaper as being seen in Goulburn at the trial of four bushrangers with whom she was friendly. By this time their father had died in Goulburn gaol while awaiting trial on a charge of murder.

Their brother James was also in prison, breaking rocks on Sydney's dreaded Cockatoo Island. He had received a seven-year sentence in January 1865 for his involvement in Ben Hall's robbery of the Cowra mail in June 1864. James was originally charged with direct involvement in this crime, but was convicted instead of being in possession of proceeds of the robbery. Thomas, too, had been associated with Hall, though he was only briefly a member of the Hall

Thomas Clarke's escape from Braidwood gaol in October 1865

gang. Probably because of his local knowledge, he seems to have been recruited by Hall for his raid on the Araluen mail on 13 March 1865.

At this time, Thomas was already on the run from the law. Almost a year earlier he had been charged with a number of offences, including highway robbery and shooting at some Chinese gold fossickers. He actually surrendered himself to police on these charges and, presumably because of this and his lack of previous convictions, he was allowed out on bail. That proved to be a costly mistake because Clarke decided to abscond and disappeared from sight, but not from the locality, as a series of attacks and robberies attested. Racehorses were stolen, mail coaches bailed up, post offices robbed and individual travellers relieved of gold and money by Thomas Clarke, in association with the Connells and others, and perhaps, but not obviously at this stage, with his younger brother, John. In these exploits they were clearly aided and abetted by their extensive network of relatives and mates.

In October 1865 Thomas Clarke was ambushed by police and taken into custody. He was held in the Braidwood gaol to await transportation to Goulburn where he would stand trial. He did not remain there long, however. With the aid of sympathisers, including, it was suspected, at least one gaol warder, he managed to scale the prison wall and escape on a horse that had been left outside for that purpose.

The depredations continued, with the police seemingly impotent to do anything about them. At times it seemed that the bushrangers had the superior tracking skills, as they carefully monitored the movements of tracking parties. In February 1866 Thomas Connell was ambushed by two policemen. The rest of the gang retaliated by capturing a policeman, thereby forcing the freeing of Connell and the surrender of the two constables who arrested him. Yet another constable who came to the rescue of his colleagues was captured and disarmed. The four police captives were then held for several hours before being released to face public shame and humiliation. Two months later the atrocities at Nerrigundah eventually brought the four undercover police volunteers in the region.

Deceit and death

The place where the bogus surveyors pitched their camp was, by design, not far from where Mary Clarke and her two daughters lived. With all the men absent or in prison the young women now carried on most of the work of the farm and often rode around the countryside where they soon made contact with the four men. At first the girls showed no suspicions and even became friendly with the newcomers. On their invitation the men even made several visits to the Clarke house where Mary Clarke persuaded them to draft and sign a petition for the release of her son, James.

It was not long, however, before the surveyor ruse became transparent as the men were seen to be keeping watch on several spots that they thought may be rendezvous points for the Clarke gang. Relations soured and were definitively ended when early in October a shot was fired into the middle of the camp, hitting no-one but giving clear warning that their real intentions had been discovered. From then on, the hunt was on in earnest.

Carroll retaliated by having people he suspected of helping the gang, including the three Clarke women, arrested. He received little help, and sometimes open antagonism, from the local police who resented the humiliation of having these interlopers amongst them. Almost all of those arrested were released for lack of evidence.

In January 1867 the partly decomposed bodies of the four volunteers were discovered in bushland near Jinden Station, south of Braidwood. It was almost universally assumed that the murders were the work of the Clarke gang, although there was also a lurking suspicion that disaffected local police were responsible. The crime was never definitively sheeted home to the bushrangers. Revenge was clearly the motive as the bodies had not been robbed. Indeed, in a macabre gesture, a 10-pound note had been inserted into the gunshot wound that had killed Carroll. It was clear too that Carroll and another of the party, Patrick Kennagh, had been 'executed', rather than killed in a shoot out, as they had been kneeling when they were shot.

The final phase

In the wake of these murders an unprecedented reward of 5000 pounds was offered for the apprehension of the murderers. By this time, John was a regular member of the gang, but several others, including the Berrymans, had been arrested and Patrick Connell had been shot dead by police.

During the following weeks crimes continued to be carried out by a newly

The surrender of the Clarke brothers. John Clarke (second from left) clasps his wounded shoulder; Aboriginal tracker, Sir Watkin Wynne (second from right) has a bandage on the wounded right arm that will later have to be amputated.

augmented Clarke gang. Internal dissension, though, bred of the constant fear of betrayal, now racked the gang and when gang member Bill Scott's body was discovered in early April 1867, it was assumed that he had been murdered by the Clarkes. As time went on, many of their former associates and helpers were now informing on them.

The end came on 26 April 1867. By this time the two Clarke brothers were alone. Acting on information from an informer, the Clarkes were traced to a rough slab hut in the vicinity of Jinden Station. A party of five police, led by an Aboriginal tracker known as Sir Watkin Wynne, surrounded the hut in the evening and waited in pouring rain for the brothers to appear. Two horses were tethered outside.

When the Clarkes came out early in the morning there was an exchange of fire before the brothers scrambled back inside, with John wounded in the shoulder. In the sporadic firing that continued throughout the morning, Sir Watkin Wynne was wounded in the shoulder, an injury that resulted in his arm having to be amputated, and the leader of the police party, Senior Constable Wright, was shot in the thigh. Early in the afternoon, police reinforcements arrived. Realising that their position was hopeless, the brothers surrendered.

They were brought to trial before Chief Justice Alfred Stephen in May for the wounding with intent to kill of Wright and Sir Watkin Wynne. In his summing up before pronouncing the automatic sentence of death, the judge delivered a cautionary homily on the futility of crime. He recited a lengthy litany of the horrors perpetrated by bushrangers throughout the 1860s and, more significantly, of the unhappy consequences that their actions had inevitably brought upon them. The Clarkes and their confederates, with their record of six murders (if Bill Scott is included), almost 40 hold-ups and innumerable other robberies, had certainly contributed significantly to the toll of death and destruction.

They went the way of most of the others mentioned in the judge's catalogue of criminals when they were hanged at Darlinghurst gaol on 25 June 1867.

FREDERICK WARD
A Self-styled Thunderbolt

As the curtain came down on the most notorious 1860s bushrangers in southern New South Wales, the centre of attention shifted to the north, where a bushranger named Frederick Ward, but known everywhere as Captain Thunderbolt, now dominated the scene. This larger-than-life character embodied, at least in the popular imagination, all the the charisma and flamboyance that the Clarkes lacked. During his lifetime, a popular ditty that did the rounds promulgated in simplistic doggerel the myth of his public-spirited altruism:

> *I'm Frederick Ward,*
> *I'm a native of this isle,*
> *I rob the rich to feed the poor*
> *And make the children smile.*

After his death, which occurred at the culmination of a furious chase on horseback across hills and gullies and into rivers—a scene that could outdo in excitement almost any modern cinematic car chase—his legend survived and thrived. Today, the doings of this larrikin robber and thief are still celebrated throughout the New England district of northern New South Wales. Immortalized in bronze, he sits proudly on horseback in the middle of the town of Uralla, near where he died. A wax effigy of the bushranger dominates the display at the local historical museum, his grave is part of the local tourist circuit and a clump of boulders, known as Thunderbolt's Rock, beside the New England Highway about seven kilometres out of town, further perpetuates his fame.

Early days and criminal beginnings

Sleek fast cars often have an irresistible attraction for the disaffected youth of today, and many a modern criminal began their lawless ways as a car thief. Horses, and especially thoroughbred racehorses, were the 19th-century equivalents of modern sports cars, and had a similar allure.

Young Fred Ward grew up around horses, and very early developed superlative riding and handling skills. He was born in about 1836 to ex-convict parents at Wilberforce, near Windsor, but at the age of about 10, he moved with his family to the Maitland area. By the time he was 17 Ward seemed to have had reasonable prospects of an honest career on the land. He and two of his brothers had obtained employment on a property known as Tocal Station in the Hunter Valley. The simple house that Ward occupied at the rear of the main station homestead still stands today. The owner of Tocal, Charles Reynolds, paid Ward the generous sum of 100 pounds a year as a horse breaker.

Frederick, in league with one of his brothers and two cousins, repaid this generosity by stealing horses from his employer and from surrounding properties, rebranding them and then taking them to Windsor to sell at auction. The provenance of the horses was soon recognised, Ward was arrested, tried and sentenced to 10 years' imprisonment on Sydney's dreaded Cockatoo Island.

He served almost half of this sentence before he was released in 1860 on a ticket-of-leave and sent to work on his sister's farm near Mudgee. It was while here that he met up with, or, more probably, resumed his childhood acquaintance with, Mary Anne Baker, who would share much of his subsequent bushranging life, bear him

Frederick Ward, alias Captain Thunderbolt

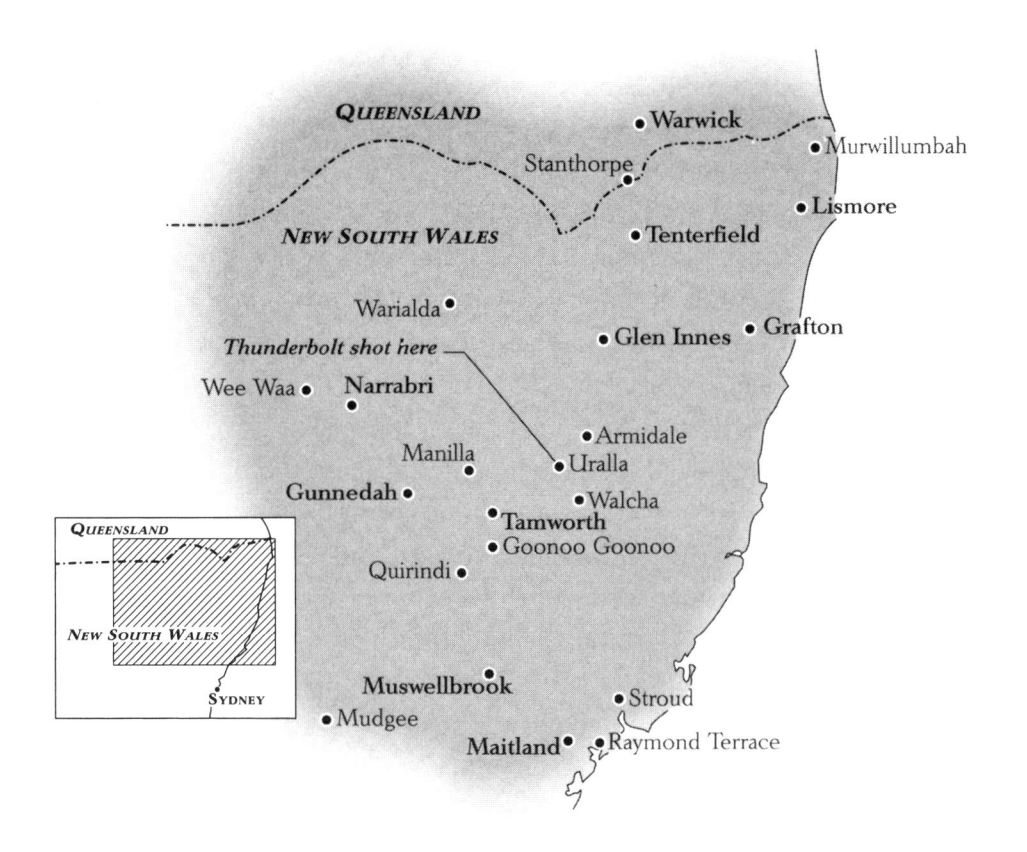

three children, eventually suffer the pain and humiliation of being abandoned by him, but survive him by almost 35 years. Mary Anne, who was known widely as 'Black Mary', became mythologised along with her lover as his constant partner in crime and as his saviour from certain capture on many occasions.

Mary Anne

Mary Anne, the daugher of James Bugg, a convict overseer of shepherds, and an Aboriginal woman, was born in 1834, near Stroud in the Hunter Valley. She lived with her parents for some years before she was taken forcibly from them and placed in the Orphan School at Parramatta, where she was trained for domestic service. She was barely 14 when she married Edmund Baker, a former policeman who by 1860 was working as a shepherd in the Mudgee district. She and the newly released Fred Ward began an affair, and in October

1861, by which time Ward was back on Cockatoo Island, she gave birth to a daughter. She registered the parents' names as Mary Anne and Frederick Ward, stating, probably falsely given her previous marriage to Baker, that the couple had been married in 1860.

In the month before the birth of his daughter, Ward was again before the courts, where he was convicted of being in possession of a stolen horse (the chances are he also stole it, but this could not be proved) and he was sent back to Cockatoo Island for another five years, plus the five remaining from his previous sentence.

It has been suggested that Ward's sense of the injustice of this conviction and further sentence fuelled his resentment and propelled him on his bushranging path. He served only two years of this second sentence before he and another prisoner, Fred Britton, managed to escape and make their way overland, first to the Hawkesbury and then to the Maitland district.

How they planned and carried out this difficult escape is not clear. One account has them hiding in a boiler on the island until they managed to slip into the water under cover of darkness and swim, hazarding the risk of shark attack, to the nearest shore at Balmain. Other versions credit Mary Anne with an active, even heroic, role in the escape. According to one of these, she herself several times braved the shark-infested waters, swimming across to deliver a file with which Ward and Britton could removed the irons which prisoners on the island constantly wore. She is also supposed to have stood on the point at Balmain, holding a light to guide the escaping prisoners.

It does seem likely, at least, that she had prior knowledge of the escape and that she was ready to provide food and clothes and to help them on their journey north. What is also probable is that she was substantially responsible for Ward's relative longevity as a bushranger—he operated continuously for seven years after his escape. Mary Anne was adept in both Aboriginal and white ways. She was able to read and write and also knew how to track and hunt in the wild. She had also trained as an Aboriginal tracker, which would obviously have enabled her to help Ward keep clear of pursuing police parties.

Whether, as legend has it, she also frequently accompanied him on raids dressed in male attire remains in the realm of speculation.

Truth or legend?

Legend often tends to ignore the obvious in idealising questionable characters such as Frederick Ward. While it is true that in his long time at large Ward never shot anybody, it is stretching credulity to claim, as some have done, that he always fired to miss. In numerous shoot-outs in which he was involved, Ward was battling for his life.

The benign solicitousness for the poor suggested in the ditty quoted above is belied by the fact that Ward often indiscriminately robbed travellers, irrespective of their wealth. According to one often-quoted story, which could be used to argue both his mean-mindedness and his generosity, Ward bailed up a band of impoverished German musicians at a place called Goonoo Goonoo, about 10 kilometres south of Tamworth. Despite their pleas, he took the 15 pounds that they had between them, but promised to return it with interest if he succeeded in bailing up a winner from that day's Tamworth races. Some weeks later the musicians received, at the forwarding address they had given Ward, the sum of 20 pounds.

It is interesting to speculate on the importance of the name Thunderbolt to the enduring legend of this bushranger. Would such a tradition have grown up around plain Frederick Ward? This romantically evocative soubriquet reportedly dates from December 1863, when Ward held up the tollgate at Campbell's Hill near Maitland. He is supposed to have told the tollkeeper, whose name was Delaney, that his name was Thunderbolt, the thunder referring to the fearsome noise he made; and the bolt to the bolt of his gun. In a further elaboration of the 'robber with a heart of gold' theme, he is also supposed to have met Delaney a little later as the latter made for a nearby public house and to have returned the money he stole from him.

A long and wide-ranging career

Frederick's Wards post-Cockatoo Island career, though centring on the New England Tableland area, which he came to know intimately, ranged over a vast area of northern New South Wales, stretching as far west as Bourke, going north over the Queensland border and extending south to the Hunter Valley. He often, thanks to his great riding skills and the magnificent horses to which he had access, was able to cover huge distances in short periods. Ward is credited with as many as 80 horse thefts, many of them of champion racehorses, more than 25 robberies of mail coaches, and dozens of raids on stations, hotels and stores. Setting aside the horse thefts, he worked up a tally of more than 70 major robberies.

Ward had hardly arrived back in the New England district when, in November 1863, he and Britton made an abortive attempt to rob a mail coach near the rock formation known as Split Rock, now renamed Thunderbolt's Rock, outside of Uralla. A shoot-out resulted in Ward's being wounded in the knee, a wound that would hinder him for for the rest of his life. This seems to have been the only incident in which Britton was involved with Ward.

Over the next seven years Ward operated in association with different groups, some of whom were extremely young and at least two of whom claimed to have been forced at gunpoint to ride with him. Soon after the incident in which he was wounded, Ward had moved to the north-west of New South Wales and, during 1864 and 1865, moved back and forth between here and the New England and Hunter regions.

In late March 1865, Ward was tracked by New South Wales police, with the help of Aboriginal trackers from Queensland, to Narran Lake, about 80 kilometres north-west of Walgett. Ward and his three accomplices—John Hogan, William McIntosh and a 16-year-old lad, John Thompson—escaped but the police captured Mary Anne, along with a quantity of stolen goods. What happened next is not entirely clear; some accounts claim that Mary Anne was taken to Walgett, where she was charged but acquitted. What seems more likely, as it concurs with a local newspaper report, is that she became ill and was left by the police at Wilby Wilby Station, about 20 kilometres to the north-east. A few days later, Ward staged a raid on the station, rescued Mary Anne and headed north across the Queensland border.

Later in the month the gang was back in the New England region, where they robbed the Warialda mail north of Tamworth, and then stole two prize horses from a nearby station at Manilla. After lying low, and travelling across country for several days, they turned up, on 24 April, at an inn owned by a Mr Munro at Boggy Creek, north of Narrabri. Here they drank heavily, helped themselves to all the money on the premises and, when the aggrieved Munro challenged them to fight, retaliated by shooting his dog. They then rode off to the tiny settlement of Millie, bailed up the innkeeper, Mr Walford, and finding no money, treated themselves to more drinks. It was while they were here that three troopers, accompanied by an Aboriginal tracker, turned up. Seeing them coming, Ward, now thoroughly inebriated, decided to take them on. The four bushrangers rode to a nearby clearing and turned to face the oncoming police. A gun battle ensued in which young Thompson was shot in the back and brought to the ground. Thompson continued to fire until he was hit again, this time in the face. Ward and his other two companions then rode off, leaving the severely wounded youngster behind. It was the first casualty that any of Ward's accomplices had suffered. Ward's appalling judgment and show of bravado in staying to fight the police was no doubt attributable largely to the amount of alcohol he had consumed. Thompson recovered from his wounds, stood trial in Tamworth and was sentenced to 15 years in prison.

As time went on and the pressures on him increased, Ward indulged to an ever greater extent his predilection for liquor. It very nearly brought him undone in December 1865. During the week before Christmas, Ward and two companions robbed three hotels. On 18 December they bailed up the hotel at Quirindi, stealing money from a group of shearers who were drinking there and staying on to drink their fill. Two days later they turned up a little further north at the inn at Currabubula, and on the afternoon of 23 December they bailed up the Griffin's Inn at Carroll, just out of Gunnedah. Here they robbed everyone, male and female, drank large quantities of spirits and, with the aid of a local fiddler, organised a dance.

At about nine o'clock in the evening, three police, attracted by the festivities but unaware of the cause of them, arrived to join the party. Recognising one of the constables, Ward beckoned his companions to follow him into a back room, which gave the landlord the opportunity to inform the newcomers of what was going on. Gunshots rang out and the bushrangers ran outside and fled into the bush, shooting the horse from beneath one of the police who attempted to give chase and wounding its rider in the arm. The party proved an expensive indulgence for Ward and his companions, who left behind their three prize racehorses and the proceeds of their robbery.

Troubles for Mary Anne, and for Ward

In May 1866 Mary Anne was arrested and charged at Stroud with vagrancy and with consorting with an escaped prisoner. Police and Aboriginal trackers had traced her and Ward to a mountain hideout where they found her with two children, one of them a baby; Mary Anne had only a few months before given birth to Ward's second child. Ward had managed to escape before the police party arrived. She was sent to gaol for six months, but was released less than three weeks later following representations on her behalf to Sir Henry Parkes, who was the New South Wales colonial secretary. The petitioner claimed that she was the victim of police harassment, a claim that seems to have been borne out when nine months later she was again arrested and charged with stealing from a shop in East Maitland. The charge was dismissed when she was shown to have purchased the goods.

Perhaps these events had contributed to a souring of Mary Anne and Ward's relationship, because sometime in late 1867 he left her and took up with a woman called Louisa Mason, the wife of Robert Mason of Aberdeen. She, like Mary Anne, was part Aboriginal and because of this was often referred to contemptuously as 'Yellow Long' or 'Yellilong'. Some months before this relationship started, and while he was still with Mary Anne, Ward had begun working with a 15-year-old youngster, Thomas Mason, who may well have been a relative of Louisa's husband; it may have been through him that he met his future lover. Ward and young Mason went to Queensland with some stolen horses, committed a number of mail coach robberies, including in May 1867 the bailing up of the Manilla mail coach.

Young Mason's juvenile bushranging career was rudely ended only months after it began. In August 1867 police came upon Ward, Mason and Mary Anne in mountainous country near Narrabri and opened fire, wounding the youngster in the shoulder. Ward and Mary Anne made good their escape, but Mason took off in another direction and was followed and captured.

Yet another young recruit of Ward's was William Monckton, who was only about 13 when he joined Ward at the end of 1867. By this time the reward for Ward's capture was a sizeable 200 pounds and he was beginning to fear betrayal by some of his contacts. Monckton was captured in 1869 when attempting to steal a horse and was sentenced at Glen Innes to a year's hard labour. He later claimed that Ward had coerced him at gunpoint to join him in his robberies. This, as well as his youth, may explain the relative leniency of his sentence. So too might the fact that he informed against William Tavenir, who was arrested near Armidale in possession of goods which he and Ward had stolen from a store nearby. Tavenir, who had joined Ward at about the same time as Monckton, was sentenced to 20 years.

Soon after this the reward for the capture of Ward was doubled to 400 pounds. Early in 1870 he supposedly admitted during a raid on a station near Manilla that he was weary of his life. He probably had reason to be. Some time before this, Louisa had become ill as a result of exposure—a direct result of the conditions she had to endure in her life with Ward. Ward had left her at a station south-west of Muswellbrook, where she died soon after. There is also reason to believe that Ward himself was seriously ill by this time, suffering from advanced tuberculosis. This came out at the inquest held after his death.

A fatal encounter

Among those who plied the roads and tracks of outback New South Wales were large numbers of itinerant hawkers who carried all kinds of wares between scattered settlements and pastoral stations. They were relatively easy prey for bushrangers and sometimes yielded rich pickings. It was, however, the robbery of an Italian hawker, Giovanni Cappisotti, for a relatively meagre haul that set in train the circumstances that led to Ward's death.

On 25 May 1870, Ward bailed up Cappisotti and a number of other travellers near Split Rock, south of Uralla, the very spot where six and a half years before, at the beginning of his bushranging career, he had been wounded in the knee while trying to rob the mail coach. Not far from here, at a spot called Church Gully, was an inn owned by a man called Blanche and his wife. Ward took Cappisotti and his other victims to the inn and demanded drinks for the company. Cappisotti asked to be allowed to leave, and Ward agreed, warning him, however, not to go to Uralla. Cappisotti left and headed south in the direction of Walcha, then, when he was well clear, changed direction and headed by a circuitous route for Uralla, where he reported Ward's whereabouts to the police. Immediately two troopers, Constable John Mulhall, who had long

136 Australian Bushrangers

been stationed at Uralla and had helped prevent the robbery of the mail coach back in December 1863, and Alexander Binning Walker, his 22-year-old assistant, set out towards Church Gully.

Back at Blanche's inn Ward had got talking to a young drover called John Cochlan, who had arrived on his employer's horse. Ward liked the look of the horse and decided to try it out. Cochlan, wisely mistrusting Ward's intentions, decided to ride along with him. When Mulhall, whose horse was faster than Walker's, arrived on the hill overlooking Church Gully, he saw two mounted horsemen. According to Mulhall's account, Ward fired at him and he returned the fire, causing his horse to bolt and its surcingle to snap. Others have suggested, less kindly, that Mulhall had pulled his horse up out of cowardice. When Walker arrived at the top of the hill, Mulhall pointed out the two horseman, both of whom he thought to be bushrangers, and the young man spurred on his horse to give chase.

Details of the chase itself are impossible to verify, as only one man survived it and we have only his word to go on. However, it seems that Ward's first impulse was to escape along the road, but that Cochlan, fearing for his employer's horse, and the consequences for himself, blocked his way. Warning the young

Constable Alexander Binning Walker, the young policeman who shot Ward after a hectic chase through rugged country.

Ward's grave at Uralla, New South Wales

drover to keep out the way, Ward had then charged off along the fence of the inn down into the valley, with Walker in hot pursuit.

All the advantages seemed to be with Walker. He was 12 years younger than his adversary who, as we have seen, was both ill and on an unfamiliar horse. Walker, too, unlike many other troopers, was an uncommonly fine horseman. The chase continued over rugged terrain, over rocks and down into valleys, with sporadic exchanges of fire. After a ride of about 10 kilometres, they arrived on the bank of Kentucky Creek. Ward drove his horse into the water, then leapt into the water and swam across. It was a fatal mistake.

Walker surprised Ward by riding after him into the water, seizing the reins of his horse, dragging it back to the bank and shooting it dead. The policeman now decidedly had the upper hand, but he had only one shot left. He spurred his horse along the bank to a spot where he could cross, only to find that Ward had managed to scramble back across to the original side. Another chase along opposite banks soon found them separated by about five metres of water. Ward stood on one side, revolver in hand; Walker sat mounted on the other, with his one remaining bullet.

There was a brief conversation in which Walker called upon Ward to surrender and he then rushed his horse into the water, where it stumbled and almost went under. Sensing his opportunity, Ward aimed his pistol and pulled the trigger, but his gun misfired. The two men then grappled in the creek, with Ward trying to dislodge Walker. At close quarters, Walker pointed his pistol at Ward and shot him in the chest. He fell into the water, mortally wounded. Walker dragged the body to the bank, tethered his exhausted horse to a tree, and then trudged back to Blanche's inn, which was only about two kilometres away. By now it was dark. Ward's body was retrieved the next morning and taken in a cart into Uralla.

Walker was honoured by the government and rewarded for his bravery by the local citizens, some of whom, however, later displayed signs of distress at Ward's burial in Uralla cemetery. The circumstances of his death were widely reported and further enhanced the Thunderbolt legend. Had Fred Ward simply expired a few months later in some lonely location from the disease that was inexorably destroying his lungs, his legend may not have long outlived him.

CAPTAIN MOONLITE
A Master Trickster

Frederick Ward, alias Thunderbolt, has been described as the last of the professional New South Wales bushrangers. His dramatic death in 1870 effectively brought the final chapter in the epic story of bushranging in the colony to its spectacular close. The Kellys were still to come but, except for one brief incursion across the border, they operated in Victoria. There was, however, to be one brief and violent appendix to the story.

Andrew George Scott's criminal career spanned 11 years, but the bushranging part of it lasted only a few days; it consisted of a single murderous rampage through a small area of the Murrumbidgee region in southern New South Wales. The whole exercise was motivated, it seems, by its leader's insane desire for public recognition and megalomaniacal need to impose his will. It was more like a crazy suicide mission than a planned raid. At times it had elements of an elaborately grotesque practical joke.

In many ways Andrew Scott seemed unlikely criminal material. He was born in Northern Ireland in 1842, the son of a Church of England minister. As his later performances conducting his own defence at his trials showed, he was well educated and capable of considerable, if often longwinded, eloquence. He even studied engineering for some time in London.

He arrived in Sydney in 1867 by, according to his own dubious account, a particularly circuitous route that had seen him involved in three wars. He claimed to have fought with Garibaldi in his Italian campaigns, and even to have been personally praised by the great man; to have joined the Union Army in the American Civil War; and to have been wounded in the leg while fighting against the Maoris at Waikato. Although subsequent events would prove Scott

Andrew George Scott, alias Captain Moonlite

to be a most plausible and resourceful liar, it is possible that this clearly deranged man came to believe many of own fabrications. He even went to the gallows maintaining, in the face of incontrovertible evidence, that he was an innocent victim of public and press prejudice. At least the wounds in Scott's legs turned out to be genuine, whatever their origin.

He moved to Melbourne in 1868 where, probably by means of forged letters of introduction, he met and ingratiated himself with the Anglican bishop. His reputation came under a brief cloud when he was named as an associate of a man accused of cattle theft, but he survived this to be appointed as a lay preacher at Mount Egerton, a thriving goldmining settlement about 25 kilometres south-east of Ballarat. It was expected that he would in time become a fully ordained minister of the church.

Scott's church stood on top of a hill overlooking the settlement. A short distance away down the hill stood the local branch of the London Chartered Bank, which was managed by an 18-year-old youth, Ludwig Brunn. Opposite the bank was the town schoolhouse. Brunn lodged with the local schoolmaster, James Simpson, who was also in charge of the Sunday school attached to Scott's church. In his first few weeks at his post, Scott gained the confidence of Simpson and Brunn and performed his clerical duties ably and conscientiously.

An unlikely bank robber

The local preacher would hardly be suspected of a bank hold-up, or so Scott calculated when he planned and executed his surprise raid on Brunn's little bank. He even managed by a clever ruse to pin the blame on his two friends.

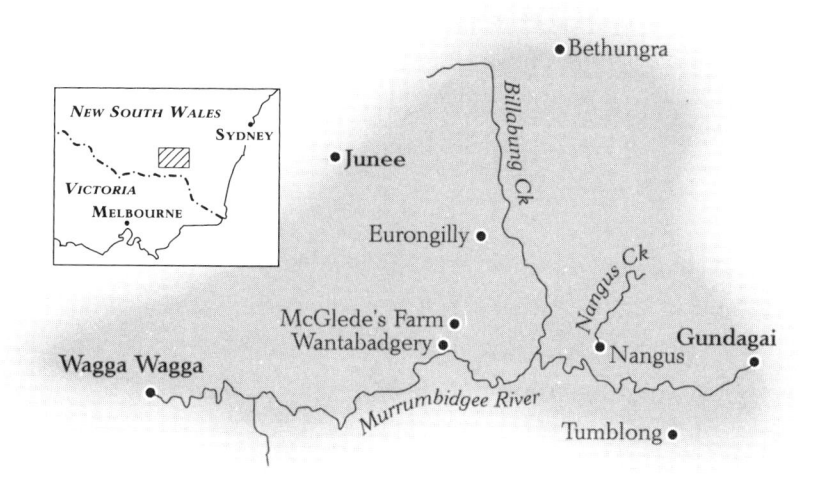

It was after dark on 8 May 1869 when, as Brunn was opening the door to his bank, he found himself confronted by a man armed with a pistol, wearing a black cloth mask and a felt hat. As soon as the man spoke, Brunn recognised the distinctive tones of Andrew Scott's Irish accent, even though he made an effort, or a pretence, of disguising them. He also recognised Scott's peculiar manner of walking as a result of the leg wounds he had received. Brunn at first took the incident to be a practical joke, until he was ordered to open the safe and hand over its contents, which comprised almost 700 pounds in cash, some gold flakes and a distinctively shaped gold bar.

Under cover of darkness, Scott then conducted his victim across the street to the schoolhouse, where he forced Brunn to write the following note: 'I hereby certify that L W Brunn has done everything in his power to withstand our intrusion and the taking away of the money which was done with firearms.' Scott then signed at the foot of the page: 'Captain Moonlite, Sworn.' Moonlite was probably a name Scott coined on the spot as a reference to the nocturnal nature of the robbery. The word 'Sworn' was in an almost indecipherable scrawl and has sometimes been interpreted as reading 'Secretary', or even 'Secret'. The name Moonlite stuck and even in official reports police used it instead of Scott. Brunn was left tied to a chair and gagged.

Scott's plan worked, at least in the short term. The local police dismissed Brunn's 'preposterous' accusation against Scott and concluded that Brunn and

Simpson had conspired to implicate him. The case against the two was strengthened when Scott confirmed that the note seemed to be in Simpson's handwriting. The two innocent men were charged with the robbery and Scott was to be a witness for the prosecution.

Arrest at sea

No doubt realising that his ruse would not stand up to closer scrutiny, Scott soon disappeared from Mount Egerton and the case against Brunn and Simpson was dropped for lack of evidence. But the stigma remained and Brunn was determined to remove it and pin the blame where it belonged. He instituted enquiries through a Sydney solicitor to trace the gold bar. The solicitor's investigations eventually established that the gold bar had been sold in Sydney by Scott for a sum of 503 pounds. By the time this information came to light Scott was already in gaol serving a 12-month sentence for forgery and theft. In late 1870 he had been chased out of Sydney Harbour and arrested aboard the luxury yacht *Whynot* he was sailing for Fiji, after having bought and refurbished it using forged credit notes and valueless cheques. Since arriving in Sydney from Egerton he had been living extravagantly beyond his means.

Scott began his sentence in Maitland gaol, but for some reason, possibly because he proved troublesome, he completed it at Parramatta after 15 rather than 12 months. He spent at least some of this time in the Parramatta Criminal Lunatic Asylum under observation after he had claimed to be suffering from hereditary insanity and refusing to eat food which he asserted was poisoned.

On his release in March 1872 he was immediately rearrested and extradited to Victoria to face trial for the Egerton robbery. His arrival at Ballarat by train was met by a large crowd, curious to catch a glimpse of the clever confidence trickster. He was placed in the new and very solid Ballarat gaol, but managed to draw further public attention to himself by contriving an ingenious escape using torn blanket strips, and freeing a number of other prisoners at the same time. He made his way to the Sandhurst diggings near Bendigo where he was traced and arrested two months later.

A long spell in gaol

By the time he was arraigned in July 1872 before Mr Justice Redmond Barry, he was quite a celebrity. He made the most of the limelight in which he found himself by dismissing his lawyers soon after the trial began and, with interminable speeches in his own defence, contriving to make the trial last more than a week. The case against him was watertight. In addition to the damning evidence of the gold bar, it also came to light that he had bought train tickets and paid off debts after the robbery using London Chartered Bank notes. Despite this, Scott regaled judge and jury with impassioned professions of his innocence, portraying himself to be the victim of a 'base conspiracy'. He eventually wound up his defence, which he clearly knew to be futile, by solemnly appealing 'to the God of Heaven, as I pass from this dock to my living tomb, that I am not guilty'. It was eloquent and, to some, inspiring, but it was all to no avail; he was sent to prison at Pentridge for 11 years, 10 for the robbery and an extra one for escaping from custody. He served seven years and was released in March 1879 after receiving remission for good behaviour. This was in spite of at least one incident in which he threatened a warder with a knife and then locked himself in a room, inveighing loudly against what he claimed to be a slander enacted against him by the *Argus*, a Melbourne newspaper. The theme of his own persecuted innocence was one Scott constantly returned to.

He came out of gaol to find himself once again a nonentity. The public taste for sensation was now being more than satisfied by news of the Kelly gang's doings. He hit on a plan to once again re-establish his public profile. He gave a series of public lectures, recounting his past, real and imagined, railing against the injustices he had been subjected to and titillating his audiences with richly embroidered tales of the horrors of life in Pentridge. The Melbourne public lapped it up for a while, but the message soon palled and the audiences fell away.

The siege at Wantabadgery

Something snapped in Scott towards the end of 1879. While in Melbourne he had attracted around him a group of five feckless young men whom he could bend to his will. The oldest of them, James Nesbitt, was 24 and had met Scott in Pentridge. The others were Thomas Rogan, aged 23; Graham Bennett, aged 20, who was from Yorkshire and the only one who was not native-born,

Gus Wernicke, aged 19; and Thomas Williams, also aged 19. They were an oddly unsuitable group to undertake any bushranging, as only Scott and Nesbitt had any skill with firearms, and at least one of them, Williams, could hardly ride a horse. We do not know on what pretence Scott led these men northwards into New South Wales in November 1879. On the way, the gang of six stole some horses and carried out some thefts, but did not attract any major attention.

On Friday 14 November, the party came to the outer reaches of the extensive Wantabadgery Station on the Murrumbidgee River, about halfway between Gundagai and Wagga Wagga. Scott went alone to the homestead and made routine enquiries about getting work. On learning from William Baynes, the station manager, that there was none offering Scott stormed off in a fury. His anger was an ominous foretaste of what was to come.

The next afternoon, Saturday, the gang of six, all armed, came back to the station, took the place over at gunpoint, forced 19 workmen into the homestead

The arrival of the Wagga Wagga police at Wantabadgery Station

dining room and demanded that the women prepare a meal. As well as the stationhands, the local postmaster and storekeeper and a visiting schoolteacher were also taken into custody. Thus began a reign of terror that was to last until the early hours of Monday morning and that was like a ghastly parody of all the previous bushranger sieges. During the next 36 hours an often demented Scott and his willing cohorts subjected their prisoners, who eventually numbered more than 30, to threats of murder and violence, a grotesque mock trial and a simulated execution. Scott basked in the power he exercised as he several times yielded, on the point of committing an atrocity, to impassioned pleas for mercy.

Real fear was first instilled early on Saturday evening when Baynes returned to the homestead. He was roughly pushed into the dining room and before the terrified onlookers told to choose how he would die, by knife or bullet. Scott prodded him repeatedly with a knife until he 'decided' to spare him. When the owners of the station, the brothers Falconer and Claude McDonald, arrived home later in the evening, they too were bailed up. Scott then imposed a midnight curfew, saying that anyone who arrived after that would be shot. This threat was, fortunately, never put to the test.

The only act of real violence during the siege occurred the next morning. A neighbour arrived to show his new thoroughbred filly to the McDonalds and was made to join the throng in the dining room. Scott mounted the frisky horse and, when it would not do his bidding, he lost his temper, took out his revolver and shot it through the head. He immediately regretted his action and expressed his sorrow for it. It was eerily reminiscent of Dan Morgan's sudden outburst during his hold-up of Round Hill Station, not far to the south of Wantabadgery, some 15 years earlier.

A trip out to gather more hostages was next on the agenda. Taking Claude McDonald and a couple of others with him, Scott rode in a buggy to a nearby hotel, the Australian Arms. As the owner was not present Scott took his wife and two children as hostages and loaded them, with the seven hotel customers, into the buggy and returned to the homestead, where he once again subjected Baynes to a humiliating and perhaps life-threatening ordeal. He had a rope with a noose thrown over a tree and announced his intention to hang the manager, whom he claimed was guilty of trying to turn his men against him.

Baynes was actually placed on the buggy with his hands tied behind him when Scott again relented in the face of pleas for clemency. The Sunday evening entertainment took the form of a mock trial. Scott sat in an improvised judge's chair, a jury was selected, and a hostage was put on trial for unlawful possession of firearms. Two stationhands acted as defence lawyers and two of Scott's men were the prosecutors. The level of debate was no doubt rudimentary, but the stationhands achieved a verdict of not guilty.

The final phase

At some stage in the evening, Scott's control slackened. In a circumstance again reminiscent of Morgan, this time his siege at Peechelba Station, one of the McDonald brothers managed to leave the house and ride to Wagga Wagga to alert the police. At about four o'clock on Monday morning, four troopers stealthily approached the station homestead, but the barking of a dog warned the bushrangers of their approach and in an exchange of fire the police were driven back, retreating to a nearby homestead.

With the police temporarily out of the way, the gang made its escape later in the morning. Along the road they met a police constable with some volunteers who were on their way to Wantabadgery and made them surrender. The enlarged group proceeded for a few kilometres until they came to a simple slab farmhouse owned by a couple named McGlede. Here they stopped, took over the house and demanded breakfast. The gang's movements had been observed and the four police from Wagga Wagga, now reinforced by five who had arrived from Gundagai and two volunteers, came to the McGlede's farm and called on the gang to surrender.

A scene of frightful carnage followed. It was a pitched battle watched by a crowd of onlookers who had taken up vantage points on a nearby hillside. In the half hour in which the bushrangers and police battled it out, Wernicke was shot in the back and mortally wounded when he rushed from the house to shoot at a policeman, and Nesbitt was shot in the head and fatally wounded when two of the troopers stormed the house. There was one police casualty. Constable Bowen, one of the Gundagai police, was shot in the neck, presumably by Scott. When the police finally stormed the house they found all the bushrangers huddling in the kitchen, with Bennett wounded in the arm. The

Constable Bowen falls, mortally wounded in the neck, during the battle between police and Moonlite's gang at McGlede's farm.

battle was over, and Scott, Bennett and Williams were captured. Rogan was not found immediately, but was later discovered cowering under a bed. Wernicke and Nesbitt died soon after. Constable Bowen was immediately promoted to senior constable. He did not get to enjoy his promotion as he died from his wound less than a week later in Gundagai.

The four surviving bushrangers were tried for murder in Sydney. Scott used all the eloquence he could muster to achieve a postponement of the trial on

The capturers of Captain Moonlite and his gang

the grounds that the publicity the incidents had generated would prejudice any jury against them. In his submission to the judge he cited the example of alleged injustices in his native Ireland, where a succession of people had been sent to the gallows as a consequence of juries that had been swayed by 'vitiated public opinion'. It was a clever argument that may have cut some ice in a present-day setting, but which was quickly dismissed then.

All four were found guilty, but a recommendation for clemency was entered on behalf of Rogan, Bennett and Williams, who were presumed to have fallen under the spell of Scott's strange charisma. Bennett and Williams, presumably because of their youth, were spared the gallows. But justice followed swiftly for Scott and Rogan, who were hanged together at Darlinghurst gaol on the morning of 20 January 1880.

The last, desperate gasp of bushranging in New South Wales had finally been stifled.

JAMES McPHERSON
The Elusive 'Wild Scotchman'

On 23 July 1895 James McPherson, who had once been Queensland's most celebrated bushranger, died just a few weeks short of his 54th birthday. He did not, like so many others of his kind, perish at the hands of the law. He met his death by accident when a horse he was riding near Burketown, just south of the coast of the Gulf of Carpentaria in far north Queensland, reared and threw him. For 20 years, since his release from prison after serving only eight years of a 50-year sentence for highway robbery, McPherson had lived in obscurity as an itinerant worker, moving around Queensland with his wife and six children, taking on a variety of droving and other jobs, and occasionally practising the trade of stone-cutting to which he had been apprenticed as a youth in Brisbane. His death went largely unremarked and he was buried in an unmarked grave in the local cemetery.

It was a strangely mundane ending for a man who had once yearned to emulate the deeds of his youthful heroes, Frank Gardiner and Ben Hall—he may well have been briefly active with Hall's gang—and who had sworn to challenge their chief persecutor, Sir Frederick Pottinger, to a duel. Yet the final years of McPherson's life were more or less consistent with the course the whole of his adult life might have been expected to follow, given his solid, albeit poor, family background, a reasonable level of education and induction at the age of 17 into the building trade.

Early years
James Alpin McPherson was born near Inverness in the Scottish Highlands in 1841, the second oldest son of a struggling family of six boys and four girls.

This illustration of James McPherson, which appeared in the Illustrated Sydney News *of 16 July 1866, was copied from a photograph taken while he was in prison awaiting trial.*

In 1854 his parents heeded the call of Australia's prominent Presbyterian patriarch, John Dunmore Lang, for Scottish people to come to the colonies to settle and work the land. They arrived in Brisbane early in 1855 and soon after moved to a property at Cresswell, about 100 kilometres inland, where they were employed as labourers. James and his elder brother, Donald, worked there as shepherds and stockmen until 1858 when the family returned to Brisbane, where James entered into a seven-year apprenticeship as a stonemason with John Petrie, a prominent local building contractor.

Despite what must have been a rather rudimentary school education, James made an impression as a literate and intelligent youth. He distinguished himself as a skilled debater in classes he attended at the Brisbane Mechanics' School of Arts. He was even reported on one occasion—though this may have been mere hearsay—to have put his powers of eloquence to good use by publicly defending the Queensland attorney-general who was being besieged by a hostile audience at a meeting in Brisbane's Fortitude Valley.

Not long after his family moved away from Brisbane in 1862, James left Petrie's service. Perhaps it was the lure of the rural life to which he was born and bred that caused him to tire of his existence in Brisbane, which was then still very much a frontier town. Very likely it was also the influence of two seasoned young law-breakers with whom he had formed a friendship and with whom he travelled north in search of work. Years later, in 1874, in a petition for his release from prison, signed by an impressive array of dignitaries, it was suggested, perhaps a little fancifully, that it was his liking for reading 'novels' that made him restless and eventually led him to crime. This habit, the petitioners maintained, filled his youthful mind with 'wild fancies' and caused him to idealise as heroes people whose influence he would otherwise have shunned. In McPherson's case, it seems, a little learning, allied to a vivid imagination, was indeed a dangerous thing!

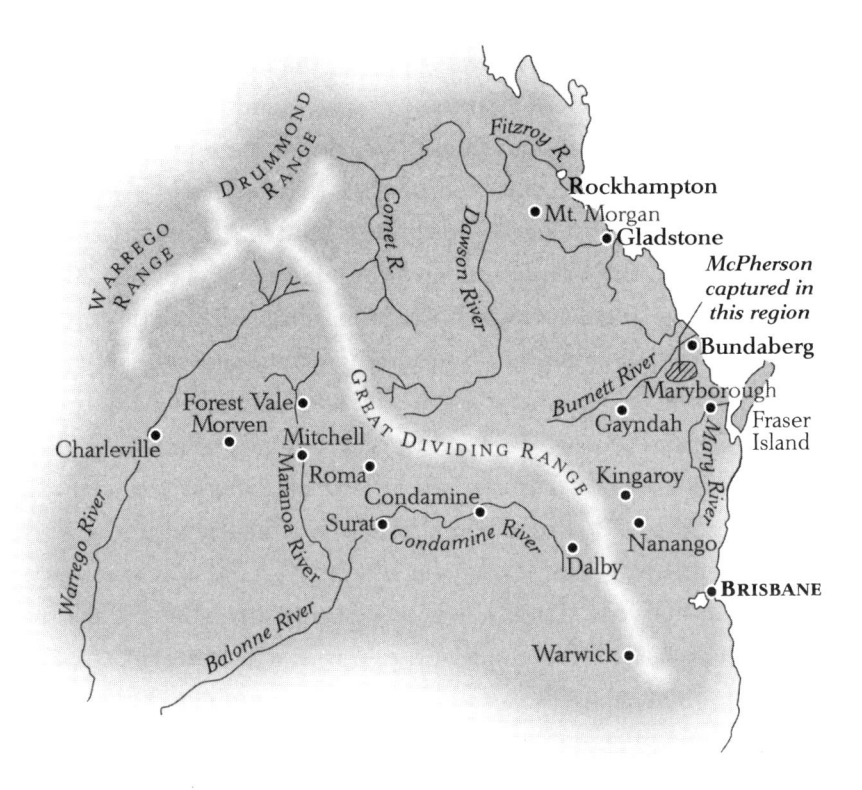

First strike

The 1874 petition for McPherson's release also tried to explain his first violent criminal act by passing it off as a reaction to an employer's injustice. By late 1863 McPherson and his two friends, Charles Dawson and Charles Morris, had worked their way, by means of short-term shearing and other pastoral labouring jobs, to a place called Reedy Creek, west of Bowen on north

Queensland's Burdekin River. Here they were dismissed by the station owner, presumably for shoddy work. When the owner refused to pay them, McPherson, so the story goes, bailed him up at gunpoint, demanded and got the wages that were owed and then cleared out with his two mates.

A little later a couple of horses disappeared from the yard of the remote Cardington Hotel, on the Houghton River, not far from where Charters Towers now stands. Dawson and Morris, who by this time was calling himself Charly McMahon, had recently started frequenting this hotel and were therefore known to the publican. So when, late in the morning of 4 March 1864, they arrived accompanied by a well turned-out stranger who introduced himself as 'Kerr', the publican, Willis, had no reason to be concerned, until he found himself confronted by Kerr's revolver pointing at his head and a demand for money and provisions.

While McPherson's attention was momentarily attracted by a remark from one of his accomplices, Willis made a move to reach for a rifle he kept under the counter. McPherson, perhaps without thinking, pulled the trigger, sending a bullet crashing into the unfortunate publican's jaw. The shot brought Willis's wife and several other people who worked about the place running. Among them were the local blacksmith and his sister. It was she who later made the connection between the man who passed himself off as Kerr and a man who called himself Alpin McPherson that she had met some months earlier.

The robbers kept the company bailed up until they had loaded their loot onto their horses and ridden off.

Southern escapades

If Dawson and Morris did in fact lead the innocent McPherson astray, he certainly ended up outdoing them in devilry. They disappeared from the scene and were never brought to justice for their part in the robbery and wounding of Willis. McPherson went on to be the scourge of the central Queensland mail service.

McPherson is supposed to have been obsessed by the doings of Hall and Gardiner. News of Gardiner's capture at Appis Creek, several hundred kilometres to the south of the Burdekin, would certainly have reached McPherson's ears and the bringing down of one of his heroes may well have added to his feelings of alienation. One of the legends that has grown up around this minor bushranger is that he is supposed to have sworn to exact revenge on Sir Frederick Pottinger by challenging him to a duel.

What is undoubtedly true is that, by the middle of 1864, and by whatever means, he turned up as a horse thief in Hall and Pottinger territory and had come to Pottinger's attention. His description and likeness had by now been widely circulated and early in August a trooper, Sergeant James Condell, accompanied by an Aboriginal tracker, recognised him riding a stolen horse on Josiah Strickland's Bundaburra Station, near Forbes in western New South Wales. Shots, all of which missed, were exchanged, but as the two law enforcers were on foot, McPherson rode off without difficulty. In the next few days there were several other sightings of McPherson, who seemed to be moving in the direction of Cowra.

Sir Frederick Pottinger now became actively involved in tracking McPherson and on 17 August he and a trooper named Towey found the outlaw at a camp near the homestead of the Walshs, Hall's in-laws, near Wheogo. The scene was set for the duel that McPherson reportedly sought. As it turned out, McPherson got the worst of it and was fortunate not to have been captured. Being caught by surprise and called upon to surrender, he immediately sprinted away, then turned and, drawing two revolvers, opened fire on the policemen who dismounted and returned it. One of Pottinger's shots hit McPherson in the left arm just above the wrist, causing him to turn and run into the bush. Pottinger and Towey followed on horseback but lost him when they were slowed down in marshy ground. Not for the first time in his career the unfortunate Pottinger was cheated of his prize.

The proximity of McPherson to the haunts and the connections of Ben Hall has led to speculation that the 'Wild Scotchman' or the 'Scotchie', as he came to be known, did indeed have direct contact with the celebrated New South Wales bushranger. While it is possible that he did, there is no hard evidence to support the theory. McPherson claimed such a connection when he next surfaced, in mid-October, hundreds of kilometres to the north-west. He must have had good connections, because on this occasion he was flamboyantly dressed and armed with a police issue rifle and revolver. He held up a settler in the mountains near Scone, fraudulently brandishing his injured arm to prove to his victim that he was an accomplice of Hall's. Later in October, still in the Scone area, he held up the mail and again escaped unchallenged.

The end for McPherson, at least for the time being, came in February 1865, when Sergeant Condell, the man who five months earlier had surprised him on Strickland's Bundaburra Station near Forbes, tracked him to a camp on the same station, took him completely by surprise and captured him without a struggle. Hall himself would later be tracked to a campsite on the same property and shot dead there, a fact that has led to speculation that the Stricklands were harbourers of Hall and his comrades. It also lends some weight to McPherson's claims that he was associated with Hall.

Escape

Although McPherson could be charged with numerous counts of robbery and one of attempted murder (of Pottinger) in New South Wales, the authorities decided to extradite him to Queensland to be tried for his crime there against Willis. He was taken to Bowen where Willis, who had now recovered from his wound, and several others positively identified him as the chief perpetrator of

Holding up the Royal Mail, the mainstay of many a bushranger's career

the outrage at the Cardington Hotel. McPherson's glib assertion that he had fired in self-defence was dismissed and he was sent to be tried at Rockhampton, almost 600 kilometres further south.

He did not arrive there. During the voyage south, aboard the paddle-steamer *Diamantina*, he persuaded the policeman accompanying him, a Constable Maher, to disobey his orders and allow him to take the air on deck. He even convinced the gullible officer that he could be trusted to go about shackled only in leg irons, without the mandatory handcuffs. By the time the *Diamantina* had reached Mackay, where it was to stop en route, Maher felt that his prisoner could be trusted. While the boat was in port, McPherson found himself hobbling unsupervised around the deck. He took his chance, slipped overboard, made it to shore, removed his leg irons with a file that he had managed to secrete in his clothes and made off into the hinterland.

It is part of the Wild Scotchman myth that he left a note pinned to a tree, thanking the Queensland government for the use of the leg irons, but stating that he no further use for them. The myth does not explain how, drenched to the skin after struggling ashore and no doubt desperate to make good his escape, he found the means or the leisure to write such a witty missive.

Full-scale bushranging

It was now September 1865 and McPherson's bushranging career, which was to last another six months, began in earnest. He almost immediately equipped himself with the basic essentials for his craft by stealing a stockman's horse, complete with saddle, as well as several pistols. He moved south and ranged over a large area of south-east Queensland, from Warwick in the far south-east to the Burnett River, just south of Bundaberg. He carried out his robberies with style and panache, usually wearing what came to be recognised as his uniform: a cabbage-tree hat—one of three that he had stolen from the Cardington Hotel—with a bright red band, and a bright red sash around his waist. He was also conspicuously well armed. Thus attired he left no-one in any doubt of his identity. He was also a garrulous robber, regaling his victims at length with stories of his exploits south of the border with Ben Hall, and contemptuously dismissing the efforts of the police to reign him in.

His first spectacular success came in mid-October when he robbed a mail coach near Condamine, making off with money and valuables to the value of 400 pounds. Several other robberies occurred in the Condamine region and then, with the hunt for him in full cry, he laid low for several weeks. In late November he moved his operations across the Great Dividing Range more than 200 kilometres to the north-east, and robbed a mail cart near the town of Gayndah.

The hunt now moved to Gayndah and was placed under the control of Inspector John Bligh O'Connell. In early December a party led by O'Connell tracked him to a gully in the nearby ranges. As O'Connell approached his quarry with his gun drawn, McPherson made a move to draw and the policeman pulled the trigger—to no avail—his pistol would not fire. He had to bear the humiliation of being held at gunpoint by the triumphant young bushranger and of being forced to retreat.

With the hunt now concentrated in the Gayndah area, the elusive McPherson moved almost 200 kilometres to the north-east where he held up the Royal Mail at the tiny settlement of Banana and then, a few days later, bewildered his pursuers again by bailing up a mailman called Paddy McCallum near Nanango, almost 300 kilometres to the south-east. McCallum later recounted how McPherson, as he sorted through the mail, had railed against the incompetence of the police, especially O'Connell, and then jocularly presented the bemused mailman with a letter to be delivered to Sir George Bowen, the governor of the colony of Queensland. Before leaving he forced McCallum to change saddles with him. Just a few days later the unfortunate McCallum was again bailed up and robbed by McPherson.

Not long afterwards, McPherson seemed to abandon even a semblance of caution when he turned up at the Gayndah Christmas race meeting on a stolen racehorse. Both he and the thoroughbred were recognised and a chase ensued in which the audacious young desperado once again left his pursuers far behind. Then, as if to push his luck to its limits, he once again lay in wait for McCallum, this time relieving him of his horse.

The end of the chase

Early in 1866 no less a dignitary than the Queensland police commissioner, David Seymour, took personal command of the hunt for McPherson. He set up his headquarters at Roma. McPherson responded by moving his operation further east to the area around Maryborough, where he continued stealing horses, robbing properties and, particularly, robbing travelling mailmen. Early in March he held up a young mailman, Edward Armitage, at Baffle Creek, north of Bundaberg.

Some time later McPherson bailed up Gin Gin Station, about 50 kilometres inland from Bundaberg, intending to steal a horse. When he found none to his liking, he enquired about the distance to the next station, Monduran, and then rode off in its direction. Soon afterwards young Armitage turned up to deliver the mail, was told of the incident and immediately identified the visitor as McPherson. Armitage and two men from Gin Gin then rode on to Monduran to warn the manager, a man called Nott, of the bushranger's impending visit. McPherson had not gone directly to Monduran and the threesome arrived before him. On hearing the news, Nott decided to take three men from Monduran as well as the three recent arrivals to head off McPherson. All except Armitage were given arms.

They sent young Armitage ahead as a decoy. Not far from the station, he came across McPherson riding slowly towards Monduran. McPherson greeted his former victim, but then caught sight of the others, who were following at some distance. Reacting quickly, he spurred his horse down a ravine by the side of the road and tried to drive it up a ridge on the other side. But his horse was tired and Nott and two of his men caught up with him in the gully and confronted him with weapons at the ready. McPherson did not call their bluff as he had so foolhardily done once before with O'Connell. He surrendered, allowing himself to be disarmed, searched, secured to his horse and taken back to Monduran homestead to await the arrival of the police.

He had not in fact given up completely. Final defeat came when, with McPherson securely chained to a tree outside the homestead, the canny Nott decided to undertake a more thorough search of his prisoner. He discovered, not entirely to his surprise, that the cunning young criminal had two small revolvers hidden deep within his clothing.

By the beginning of April 1866 he was in gaol in Maryborough. He was transferred to Brisbane, this time securely shackled all the way, to stand trial for the wounding and robbery of Willis at the Cardington Hotel. At his trial, which took place in August, his defence lawyer, citing the length of time that had elapsed since the alleged assault, was able to challenge the accuracy of Willis's and other prosecution witnesses' recollection of the events and even suggested that the discharge of McPherson's pistol was a result of the 'mere nervous trembling of the prisoner's finger'. The jury accepted his argument and returned a verdict of not guilty.

At least McPherson had escaped a possible death sentence, but there were other charges to answer, ones much more difficult to refute. In September 1866 he appeared in Maryborough court to face two charges of armed robbery. On these he was found guilty and sentenced to two consecutive terms of 25 years.

The successful 1874 petition for McPherson's release stated as one of its arguments that McPherson had by then served eight years, 'during which time he has, with one exception, conducted himself in a most exemplary manner'. That one exception might well, in less sympathetic times, have put paid to any hope of freedom.

Early in 1870 he was transferred to the prison fortress on the island of St Helena in Moreton Bay. Not long afterwards, he and five other prisoners escaped from the prison compound by rushing a warder. They were all promptly recaptured before they could leave the island.

Four years later, this one blot on his prison copybook was not held against him.

HARRY POWER
A Victim of Betrayal

In 1853, the Success, *moored in an inlet in Port Phillip Bay, was pressed into service as a convict hulk to relieve the overcrowding that a gold-inspired crime wave had brought to the prisons in the colony of Victoria. The* Success, *and its sister hulk, the* President, *accommodated the goldrush bushranger Frank MacCallum, alias Captain Melville, in the 1850s and it was during a visit to the prisoners held on the* Success *in 1857 that John Price, the Victorian inspector-general of convicts and former commandant of Norfolk Island, was brutally battered to death. Years later, in November 1891, and long after it had ceased to be a prison, the* Success *was indirectly responsible for another death—that of Harry Power, one of the last surviving Victorian bushrangers, and a man widely thought to have been a mentor for the young Ned Kelly.*

Attracted by the lure of gold, Harry Power had come to Victoria from Ireland in the early 1850s. In March 1855 he fell foul of the law when he shot and wounded a trooper who had stopped him on suspicion of riding a stolen horse. For this offence he was sent to Pentridge Prison for 14 years. Only months before he was due for release, he escaped while he was transferring rubbish from the prison to a dumping ground outside. He made his way to north-eastern Victoria and for the next year or so he lived as a bushranger, hiding away in a mountainous region of the King River valley. He was captured after being betrayed by a trusted friend, brought to trial and sent back to Pentridge to serve a further 15 years. For some time it was speculated that it was Ned Kelly who informed on him. Just a month before Power was caught, Kelly was arrested and charged with being an accomplice in some of Power's robberies. While there seems no doubt that the 15-year-old Kelly was an associate of Power, he was acquitted for lack of evidence, and was later shown to have played no part in his friend's capture.

At about the same time that Power emerged from prison in the mid-1880s, the Victorian government sold the *Success* to some enterprising entrepreneurs who set it up as a kind of 'living' convict museum, complete with life-like wax models of the prisoners confined to its gloomy interior. As a customer-attracting gimmick, the amiable, talkative old Harry Power was employed as a living exhibit. Harry's job was to entertain visitors with accounts of his bushranging and convict experiences, and by all accounts he was good at it.

After being exhibited in Melbourne and then in Hobart, the *Success*, with Harry Power, was brought to Sydney where it opened for some time at Circular Quay. A trip to England was planned and the ship was moved elsewhere in

Sydney Harbour to be fitted out for the voyage. While it was here, it was sabotaged in the dead of night by a group of people who objected to the commercial exploitation of a cruel convict past and it sank at its moorings. It was salvaged but had to undergo extensive refurbishing and repairs. While these were being carried out, Power took himself south, near to his former stamping ground, for a recuperative holiday. On 7 November 1891, while he was fishing on the marshy banks of the Murray River near Swan Hill, the former bushranger and long-time prison inmate fell into the river and drowned.

A year at large

Power had escaped from Pentridge on 7 May 1869. He made his way quickly to the north-eastern highlands where he announced his arrival in spectacular fashion by holding up the Cobb & Co mail coach at Porepunkah, just north of Bright. He carried out a number of other mail robberies in the area and then, as pressure from increased police activity took its toll, moved over the border into the Monaro district of southern New South Wales. Lack of contacts here caused him to return to Victoria in late September, where he took refuge in the mountainous region in the upper King River region. From here he came down at regular intervals to carry out his raids on settled areas. He relied heavily on contacts and associates who included, probably, members of the Kelly family who lived in Greta. As a local newspaper lamented, 'From a certain section of the local population ... [Power] has received succour and information, while the police have been deceived.'

Networks, as Power discovered to his cost, are essential to anyone on the run, but they can also be dangerous. Power was sheltering in a remote part of the upper King River valley in a primitive hut on the property of a small-time farmer named James Quinn. Quinn was Ned Kelly's grandfather; his daughter, Ellen, married the Irish ex-convict John Kelly in 1850. Obviously a number of sympathisers knew the location of this hideout. One of them was a man named Jack Lloyd, who had first met Power in Pentridge while he was serving a five-year sentence for cattle theft. Lloyd and his brother, Tom, were both uncles by marriage of Ned Kelly. They each married daughters of Quinn, sisters of Ellen Kelly. Lloyd was on friendly terms with Robert McBean, the owner of a station near Benalla. Power made the mistake of raiding McBean's property and stealing, among other things, a watch to which McBean attached great sentimental value. When McBean told Lloyd of his loss, the latter admitted his connection with the robber and offered to broker a deal for the watch's return. McBean, however, informed the police of Lloyd's link with Power. The police in turn approached Lloyd, offering a substantial reward for information about Power's hiding place. Lloyd agreed.

Accordingly, in late May 1870, a party led by Lloyd and comprising police superintendents Nicolson and Hare, both of whom would later figure in the hunt for Ned Kelly, and an Aboriginal tracker, headed south from Wangaratta. The weather was wet and cold and the party made heavy going of the journey, taking three days to reach their destination and running out of provisions on the way. They arrived hungry and in a state of near exhaustion.

One of the usual advantages of Power's hideout was a peacock on Quinn's farm which habitually set up a loud screeching at the approach of strangers. For some reason, however, it abandoned this habit on this crucial occasion and allowed the police party to sneak up to Power's lean-to and surprise him while he slept.

The captured bushranger, once over his initial shock and annoyance, showed some magnanimity in defeat. Seeing the reduced state of his captors, he generously indicated to them the location of his larder and offered them the hospitality of his humble lair. He may also, of course, have calculated that his chances of arriving back in Wangaratta alive would be enhanced if those escorting him did not perish on the way.

When Power, mounted on horseback and escorted by the police party, reached Wangaratta in the early evening of 5 June, a crowd had gathered to watch the arrival of the bearded, burly bushranger. He is reported to have conducted himself with dignity, acknowledging the waves of the people and, trying to depict his misfortune in the most favourable light, assuring those within hearing that he had been captured while asleep.

Two days later, as he was being transferred to the gaol in Beechworth, he once again briefly enjoyed the limelight as a motley gathering of well-wishers, antagonists and sensation-mongers accompanied the cart that carried him into the town.

He was arraigned for four robberies, all of them committed in the area that

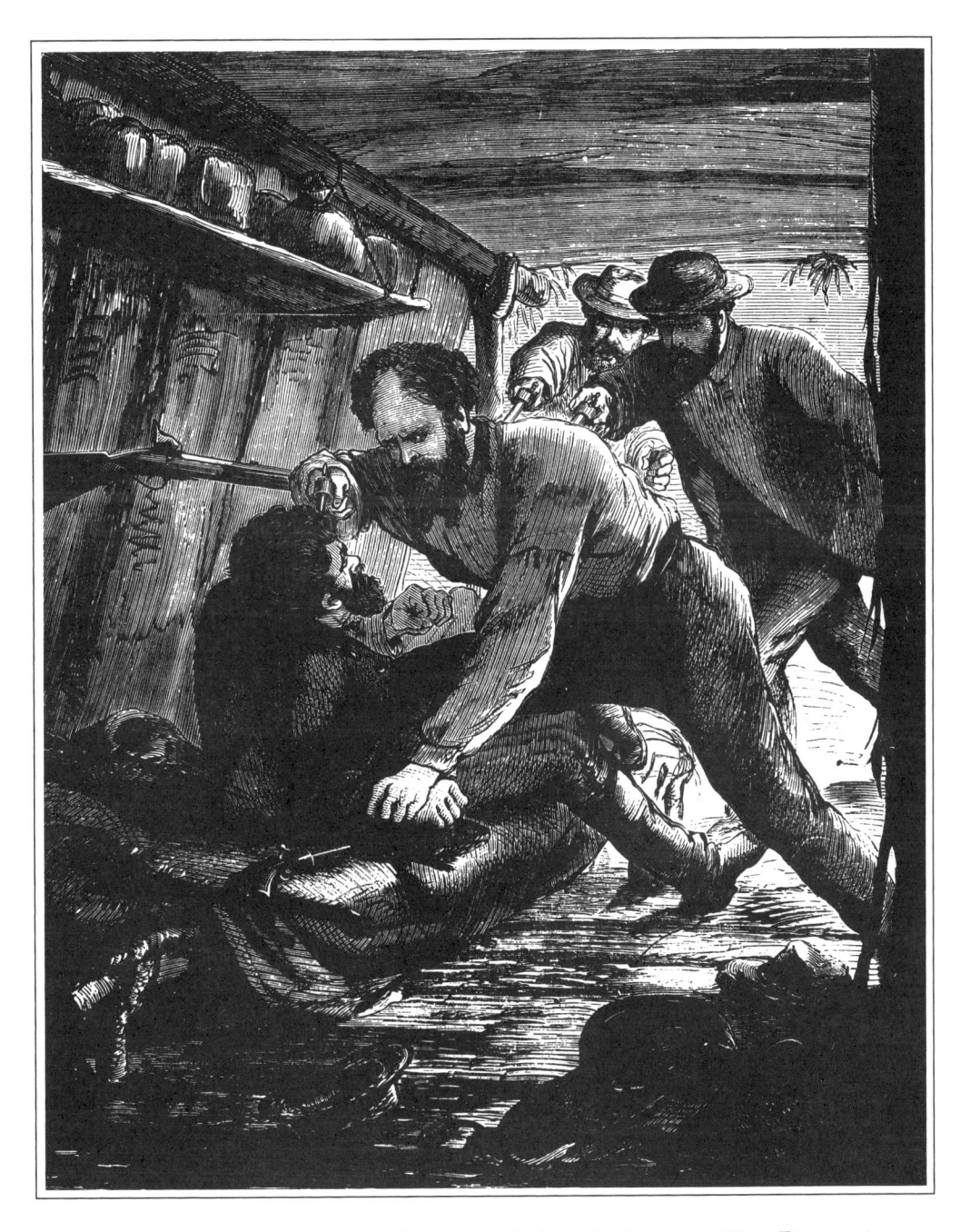

The capture of Harry Power in his remote hideout in the upper King River region

Harry Power in Pentridge prison during the 1870s

would later become known as 'Kelly country'. Three of the charges involved the bailing up of individuals; the other concerned the robbery of the Beechworth mail coach. Apart from some gruff, hectoring threats, Power had not resorted to violence in any of these robberies, and had, luckily for him, never been involved in a shoot-out.

His trial took place in October 1869 and he was found guilty on all counts.

THE KELLY GANG
Everlasting Folk Heroes

Australia's last and most celebrated bushranger, Ned Kelly, may have developed into no more than the quarrelsome, petty criminal and intermittent gaolbird that he already was had an inebriated policeman not made an unscheduled visit to the Kelly's small slab hut late on the afternoon of Monday 15 April 1878.

Constable Alexander Fitzpatrick had come to arrest 17-year-old Dan Kelly on a charge of horse stealing. Ned, who was 23, was also wanted, but was thought to be out of the area. Indeed, he later claimed that he was far away at the time. By going to the hut Fitzpatrick was disobeying strict orders that no policeman was to approach the troublesome Kelly household unaccompanied. Fizpatrick knew Ned Kelly well and had a score to settle with him. Eight months earlier he had arrested Ned one evening in Benalla for being drunk and disorderly. It has been suggested that Fitzpatrick had been drinking with the young ruffian and had set him up by spiking his drink. The following morning, as Fitzpatrick and another policeman, Constable Lonigan, were taking him to the courthouse, Kelly lashed out and floored Fitzpatrick with a punch before he was eventually subdued and unceremoniously carried to the court. He was fined four pounds six shillings.

What happened during the rest of the April 1878 evening is a matter of claim and counterclaim. What is certain is that Fitzpatrick, smelling strongly of brandy, turned up the next morning at Dr John Nicholson's place at Benalla to be treated for two wounds to his left wrist which, according to the doctor, 'might have been produced by a bullet'. Fitzpatrick's version of what happened was accepted by the authorities, although his record and his later dismissal

166   Australian Bushrangers

from the police on the grounds that 'he could not be trusted out of sight' must make it highly questionable.

Fitzpatrick claimed that soon after his arrival Ned Kelly burst into the hut and fired at him and Ellen Kelly, Ned's mother, then hit him over the head with a shovel. A second shot from Kelly at point blank range hit him in the left wrist and when he reached to draw his revolver, he found that Dan Kelly had removed it from the holster. Ned is also supposed to have fired a third shot, which went astray. Fitzpatrick also asserted that while this was going on, two other men, William Williamson and William Skillion, had appeared with revolvers in hand at a bedroom door. Skillion was the husband of Maggie, the eldest of Ellen Kelly's three surviving daughters; and Williamson was a neighbour of the Kellys. Fitzpatrick claimed that when things had settled down, he, assisted by Ned Kelly, removed the bullet with a penknife, thus creating the second wound. He was, according to his account, detained at gunpoint until eleven o'clock, when he was allowed to leave.

Two farmers gave evidence that Skillion was with them at the time of this episode, but their word was discounted in favour of Fitzpatrick's. In 1881 a royal commission held to review the events of the Kelly outbreak, and particularly the performance of the police, found that Williamson had not been present and granted him a retrospective pardon.

In the wake of this incident Ellen Kelly, William Williamson and William Skillion were arrested on the charge of aiding and abetting Ned Kelly in the attempted murder of Fitzpatrick and placed in Beechworth gaol. Ellen's recently born infant daughter, Alice, went to prison with her.

On 9 October the case came before Judge Sir Redmond Barry at Beechworth. The three were found guilty. Williamson and Skillion were sentenced to six years' hard labour and Ellen Kelly to three years in prison. In sentencing Ellen, the judge, in a surprising departure from legal protocol, informed her that if her son Ned were there, he would happily send him to prison for 15 (some accounts say 21) years. The same judge would, two years later, impose a much more drastic penalty.

When their mother came to trial, Ned and Dan, who now had a price of 100 pounds on their heads, were ensconced away to the south in their hideaway campsite at Bullock Creek, close to Stringybark Creek in the Wombat Ranges. Their future course had one overriding aim—to have their mother released from prison and to establish her innocence.

A delinquent childhood

Ned Kelly, and indeed the Kelly family generally, had had many brushes with the law before the incidents which saw Ellen sent to prison and made fugitives of Dan and Ned. At the time of their mother's conviction, their brother, Jim, who was two years older than Dan, was in prison serving a five-year sentence for cattle stealing. He was 14 when he was convicted and his imprisonment probably saved him from following his brothers to their eventual doom. Ellen herself, a small but doughty and aggressive woman, had previously tangled with the law when, in 1865, she had been fined two pounds for abusing and threatening a neighbour. She had also been in trouble on charges of illicit grog dealing.

Ned Kelly had criminal antecedents on both sides of the family. His father, John Kelly, known as 'Red' Kelly because of his bushy red beard, was transported to Tasmania for seven years from his native Tipperary in 1842. He was 21 when he was sentenced and is generally thought to have been convicted of pig stealing. He moved to Victoria after he was released and in November 1850 he married Ellen Quinn in St Francis' Catholic church in Melbourne. Ellen, who was 18 when she married Kelly, was the daughter of James Quinn, who had come to Melbourne as a free settler in 1841 from County Antrim in Ireland. During the 1850s, two of his sons, Jimmy and Jack, were several times charged with cattle theft and the family was the object of constant police surveillance. It was Quinn who harboured Harry Power on his property, called Glenmore, in the upper King River valley.

Like most of the selector class to which they belonged and which would later provide Ned with his network of sympathetic supporters, the Kellys lived in grinding poverty. Ned, the couple's third child, but only the second to survive beyond infancy, was born at Beveridge on the northern outskirts of Melbourne in November or December 1854. When he was six the family moved further north to Avenal, between Seymour and Euroa, where they rented a 40-acre (16-hectare) farm. Ned attended school at Avenal where he became reasonably proficient in reading and writing. When he was only nine he showed some sign of the courage and strength that he later displayed in abundance when he rescued a school mate, Richard Shelton, from drowning in a swiftly flowing creek. He was awarded a green sash for this act of heroism. He must have cherished it because he was wearing it when he was captured at Glenrowan.

It was while the family was at Avenal that Ned's ailing father was convicted, in 1865, on a dubious charge of possessing a stolen cowhide. As he could not raise the fine of 25 pounds that was imposed, he was put in gaol at Kilmore, about 60 kilometres to the south-west, until the money was found. He died just after Christmas the following year from complications arising from the dropsy he had been suffering for some time. Ned, at 12, was now the oldest but one of a family of seven children. His elder sister, Annie, who was to die in childbirth almost exactly six years later, was barely a year older than he.

In 1867 Ellen Kelly moved her family to the 88-acre (36-hectare) selection at Eleven Mile Creek, near Greta. It was about two years after this that Ned's troubles with the law began. He spent a week in gaol while awaiting trial on a charge of assaulting and robbing a Chinese gold fossicker, Ah Fook, before being released when the case against him could not be substantiated. At about this time, too, he came under the influence of the rough-and-ready, but avuncular, escapee from Pentridge, Harry Power, who had just arrived in the region and who enlisted the aid of the willing young lad in a series of robberies. Early one morning in May 1870 a police party descended on the Kelly homestead and arrested 15-year-old Ned on suspicion of being associated with Power. He was thrown into gaol at Benalla, where he remained for about a month while the police tried, unsuccessfully, to get him to give information about Power's whereabouts. The charges were dismissed, once again for lack of concrete evidence. Not satisfied with this, he was gaoled in Kyneton, where a Superintendent Nicolson once again endeavoured to get him to betray Power. Eventually he was released when a court failed to convict him.

The next charge against Ned Kelly, which was brought about four months later, earned him a six-month sentence. Encouraged by a hawker named Gould with whom he was friendly, Ned took a parcel containing calves' testicles to the wife of another hawker, called McCormack, with whom he and Gould were having a dispute and whom Kelly was alleged to have assaulted. The point of this crude practical joke was that the woman was childless as a result of her husband's impotence. Six months was a harsh sentence for what was little more than an insensitive act of larrikinism which, moreover, was probably at least as much Gould's idea as it was Kelly's.

Ned was hardly out of Beechworth gaol, after serving four of the six months, when he was again arrested, this time with a provocative display of police violence. He was riding through Greta township on a mare that a mate of his, known as Wild Wright, had temporarily appropriated some time before, while Ned was still in prison. It was common practice for these unruly country youths,

Ned Kelly's prison record

in a gesture of defiance and bravado, to 'borrow' fine horses from local wealthy squatters; they did not consider it theft as the horses were usually returned. Unfortunately for Kelly, Wright had lost the horse and Ned had happened upon it. It is not clear exactly what he intended to do with it, but it does seem that he was guilty of at least a degree of provocation as he rode the mare conspicuously through Greta several times until Senior Constable Hall, a hulking, brutish character, finally noticed him.

Hall approached the mare on foot, seized Kelly by the arm and wrestled him to the ground. Kelly was by now a tall, strong youth of 16, and approaching his final height of just under two metres. As Hall manhandled him, he fought back vigorously. At this point Hall drew his revolver and, aiming it at his adversary's head, pulled the trigger several times. Fortuitously, the gun failed to fire. By now the flailing 16-year-old was being held down by a number of men who had come to Hall's assistance. Hall then took his revolver by the barrel and began to beat Kelly mercilessly around the face and head with the butt, drawing blood and rendering Kelly almost unconscious. It was a cowardly display—and one which Hall made no attempt to deny—but it lost him no kudos with his Kelly-hating colleagues, or with the local wealthy squatters, whose security was threatened by the likes of the Kellys and other disaffected selector families.

A few months later, at the beginning of August 1871, Kelly was brought to trial at Beechworth on the trumped-up charge of horse theft. When this, for obvious reasons, could not be made to stick, he was recharged with being in possession of a stolen horse. He was found guilty, and sent to Pentridge for three years, with some of the time to be spent on the prison hulks *Success* and *President* in Port Phillip Bay.

When he was released in February 1874, his younger brother, Jim, had already been in prison for 10 months and his mother was about to marry a Californian gold prospector, George King, who was only about five years older than Ned.

During the next three and a half years, until his altercation with Constable Fitzpatrick in Benalla in June 1877, Kelly had no encounters with the law, possibly because he spent much of the time far removed from his former haunts. He was almost certainly involved, however, for at least some of this time in illegal activities. One of his first exercises in law-breaking after his release brought him a great deal of local notoriety and firmly established his reputation for physical strength and bravery. It has been claimed that it marked the beginning of his status as a local hero. Bare-knuckle boxing, which had been a popular sport and public spectacle in the early gold-digging days, had been illegal in Victoria since the introduction of the Queensberry rules in the mid-1860s. Despite this proscription, these fights were still held in secret places, watched by large crowds, and wagered on by many more. Soon after his release, Kelly was matched with his former mate Wild Wright, whom Ned felt was responsible for his long imprisonment. In a gruelling 20-round contest Kelly vanquished his opponent to the plaudits of the local populace.

Kelly was an itinerant for much of the next three years. He spent some time panning for gold in the King River region in company with George King, worked at a timber mill in Mansfield long enough to become foreman, and went sheep-shearing in the Riverina area of New South Wales. From about mid-1876 he and his stepfather, along with some other relatives, also began to operate a horse-stealing racket, taking horses from around the Benalla region and transporting them to a hideout in the Wombat Ranges, from where they could be sent to Melbourne to be sold.

It was during this time that Ned became intimately acquainted with the mountain country in which he would take refuge after the incident which led to his mother's arrest.

Friends, supporters and sympathisers

There was a strong sense of class solidarity among the selectors of north-eastern Victoria—many of them were failed gold diggers who, after the passing of the Victorian Land Acts of the 1860s, had taken up small holdings on which they tried, often with little or no expertise and on land that was not congenial to farming, to eke out a living. Their presence was resented by the powerful and now wealthy squatters who had arrived in the area 30 to 40 years earlier and who objected to any diminution of the area they controlled. Conflict between squatters and selectors was endemic and in disputes the law-enforcing authorities generally favoured the more powerful and politically influential squatting interests.

Dan Kelly *Kate Kelly*

The Kellys were poor selectors and a tearaway youth such as Ned was easily perceived by others of his class, perhaps with some justification, as an innocent victim of official harassment. It was certainly a line that Ned himself later pushed at great length in his self-justificatory haranguing speeches to his captive audiences at Euroa and Jerilderie, and in two lengthy documents that he tried, unsuccessfully, to have published. When Ellen Kelly was arrested and Ned and Dan fled to the mountains, public sympathy in the area was strongly on their side. It has been estimated that they enjoyed the active support of more than 800 local settlers during their time at large.

More immediately significant, however, was the practical help the brothers received from a circle of close friends and relatives who brought them supplies and kept them informed of police activities and movements. Prominent among these were their older sister, Maggie, Skillion's wife, and their younger sister, Kate, who was only 16 when her brothers went into hiding. Wild Wright continued to be a friend despite his mauling four years earlier at Kelly's hands.

Ned's closest friend and ally at this time was Joe Byrne who, at 21, was little more than two years Ned's junior. He had first met Kelly some time in 1876 and had become a firm admirer of his. Like his friend he was tall and goodlooking; he was also a superlative horseman, probably the best of any of the Kelly gang. He was, like Kelly, from an Irish Catholic family which ran a dairy farm at a place called Woolshed just a few kilometres north of Greta. A school friend of Byrne's, who, until he later turned police informer, was a close associate of his and the Kellys, Aaron Sherritt, who had earlier served a six-month sentence with Byrne when they were jointly convicted of stealing meat.

Steve Hart was a particular friend of Dan Kelly. Born in 1859 at Beechworth, he was only 18—two years older than Dan—when the Kellys were forced to take to the hills. He was a short, slightly built young man with a penchant for flash clothes and a tendency to show off. He, too, was an accomplished horseman, who from time to time had ridden at race meetings. His love of horses had gotten him into trouble in 1877 when he spent 12 months in Beechworth gaol for horse stealing.

Stringybark Creek and the forming of a gang

An unfortunate coincidence forced Byrne and Hart to become members of the Kelly gang. Indeed, until the fateful events of 26 October 1878, there was no Kelly gang as such, merely a loose-knit collection of helpers. Byrne and Hart just happened to be the two helpers who were present when Ned Kelly discovered a police party camped on Stringybark Creek, not far from his camp at Bullock Creek in the Wombat Ranges, where the brothers passed their time searching for gold.

The plan to entrap the Kelly brothers in the Wombat Ranges was approved by Superintendent Sadleir, who was stationed at Benalla. The police knew of their location thanks to information supplied by a squatter who had spotted them close to Stringybark Creek. Sadleir's idea was that two police parties travelling from opposite directions, one going south from Greta and the other coming north from Mansfield, would be able to surround the two outlaws and capture or kill them. Their intention to kill the brothers if necessary was evidenced by the fact that strong straps capable of carrying a dead body on each side of a packhorse were included among both parties' equipment. A friend in Greta who had got wind of the expedition managed to inform the Kellys, so the brothers were alerted to at least one of the parties that was on their trail.

On the morning of 25 October 1878, just 16 days after Ellen Kelly began her prison sentence, four policemen and a packhorse with provisions and equipment to transport dead bodies left Mansfield. That evening, after climbing into the ranges and traversing a distance of about 30 kilometres, they set up camp on one of the banks of Stringybark Creek. All four were Irishmen. At their head was Sergeant Michael Kennedy, who was 37 years old and had come to Victoria 19 years earlier. He had been stationed at Mansfield for almost 15 years. Also in the party was Constable Thomas Lonigan, 37, who had tangled with Ned Kelly 18 months earlier at Benalla when he was under arrest for drunken and disorderly behaviour and against whom Kelly bore an abiding grudge. Both Lonigan and Kennedy were married and had children. The other two, who were both unmarried, were Constables Michael Scanlon, 36, and Thomas McIntyre, 32.

Early on the morning of 26 October Kennedy and Scanlon left the camp to reconnoitre for signs of the Kellys, leaving Lonigan and McIntyre behind. Somewhere about midday, McIntyre went off into the bush to investigate a noise, but found nothing. On the way back, possibly in an unguarded moment, he made a mistake that would cost his colleagues their lives—he took a potshot at some parrots. The Kellys, with Byrne and Hart, heard the gunshots and set out in the direction from which it came to investigate. Meanwhile McIntyre, sensing no danger, returned to the campsite and carelessly threw his rifle into the tent. By mid-afternoon McIntyre and Scanlon further advertised their whereabouts by lighting a large fire. Their purpose was to help guide their colleagues, whom they feared had lost their way, back to the camp; the effect was to bring their four adversaries to the edges of their camp, where they could observe the two policemen. They were not in uniform, but Kelly could have had no doubt of what they were about as he clearly recognised Lonigan.

As in the case of the Fitzpatrick incident, the exact details of the gun battle that followed are difficult to piece together. The only account we have, apart from Kelly's, is the one that McIntyre gave. It is no doubt substantially true, but given the circumstances under which McIntyre observed the events, and some of the medical evidence presented at the trial on the condition of the bodies, some of the details are open to question.

According to McIntyre, about five o'clock in the afternoon, with rain

176   Australian Bushrangers

*Lonigan lies dead as the camp at Stringybark Creek
is surrounded by the Kelly gang.*

threatening, he and Lonigan were standing on opposite sides of the fire sharing a billy of tea when a call to 'bail up' was heard from the edge of the campsite. McIntyre turned round, saw four men with rifles trained on him and his colleague and, having no weapon handy, raised his hands in the air. Lonigan, however, ran towards a log and attempted to crouch behind it as he drew his revolver. Kelly, whose rifle was trained on McIntyre, swung around and fired. The shot hit Lonigan in the eye, causing him to cry out 'Christ, I'm shot!' before he collapsed and died.

McIntyre was then instructed to remain in the middle of the campsite and await the return of Kennedy and Scanlon. The four bandits, all of them now implicated in murder, retired to the bushes with their guns trained on him. McIntyre had agreed to advise his colleagues to surrender with a promise that if they did so they would be allowed to leave unmolested, minus their weapons and horses.

About half an hour later, the unsuspecting Kennedy and Scanlon rode calmly into camp. As Kennedy approached, McIntyre shouted out to him that they were surrounded and at the same time Ned Kelly called out. Taken by surprise, Kennedy instinctively went to draw his revolver, then threw himself to the ground as a rifle shot rang out. Shielding behind his horse, he exchanged shots with the outlaws and then started to duck and weave his way towards the shelter of some trees.

Scanlon was dismounting when the firing had started. As soon as he was on the ground he tried to gather up his rifle which had been slung over his shoulder, but was hit just below the right shoulder and collapsed, mortally wounded. McIntyre, sensing that the gang's attention was now focused on his colleagues and having no weapon of his own, leapt onto Kennedy's horse and spurring it into a gallop managed to ride clear of the camp and into the bush.

McIntyre arrived in Mansfield the next afternoon, soaked, bleeding and in a state of near collapse, to tell his terrible story. In the early hours of the next morning, a search party set out for the campsite. They found the bodies of Lonigan and Scanlon, but could find no trace of Kennedy. Perhaps, it was thought, he was still alive and had been taken hostage. Any such hopes were dashed three days later when Aboriginal trackers led searchers to his body, covered with a rain sheet—the rains had come on soon after the massacre— and lying several hundred metres from the camp.

In the wake of this incident, the Victorian government passed it own Felons Apprehension Act, similar to the New South Wales one of 13 years earlier. The Kelly gang were declared to be outlaws and a total reward of 3000 pounds was offered for their apprehension, dead or alive. At this stage, only two of the gang, the Kelly brothers, had been positively identified.

We have only Ned Kelly's description, given at his trial, of what happened after McIntyre made his escape. As he recounted it—and his account does seem to tally with the evidence—Kennedy fired wildly as he stumbled towards some trees, two of his bullets grazing Ned and another hitting Dan. As he ran through the scrub trying to take cover, he was hit in the shoulder by a shot from Ned Kelly. He turned and, as Kelly believed, was about to fire, when another of Kelly's shots struck him in the chest. The most contentious part of Kelly's evidence concerns the last shot fired. He claimed to have spoken to

Kennedy for some time and then, seeing that he was clearly dying and wishing to spare him further pain, finished him off with a bullet through the heart.

It is not entirely clear whose shot killed Scanlon but, as his ring was found on Byrne's finger after the Glenrowan massacre, it was probably his.

Lone witnesses to terrible events are apt to have their veracity doubted, especially if a taint of dishonour could attach to the part they played. And so it was with McIntyre. His actions in shooting at birds and lighting fires had been injudicious at best, and it was inevitable that the circumstances of his escape should be called into question. However, the only real discrepancy was between his evidence and later findings related to Lonigan, who was found to have four wounds, rather than the single one that McIntyre described. It was confirmed, however, that it was a shot through the eye that almost certainly caused his death.

No doubt traumatised by these events, the gang, for that's what circumstances had decreed they now were, struck northwards through the pouring rain, hoping to cross the Murray River into New South Wales. When they reached the river they found its waters swollen by the downpour and were forced to retreat back into Victoria.

A passion for vindication

Ned Kelly was now a murderer; so too, probably, was Joe Byrne, and in the eyes of the law Dan Kelly and Steve Hart also had blood on their hands. It is unlikely, though, that any of them had murder on their minds when they came upon the police camp; had there been no resistance, the three dead policemen would probably have been alive and held in disgrace, rather than dead and hailed as heroes. It was of course ingenuous of Kelly and his accomplices to imagine that they could take the camp without a battle, just as it was naive of him to believe, as he seemed to, that he would be able to justify his actions to an understanding public.

Kelly had a passion for self-vindication and an obsession with publicising his cause and it is arguable that it was this passion, much more than the usual motives for robbery, that prompted his raids on Euroa and Jerilderie. On both these occasions he not only harangued his captive audiences in his own defence, but he left behind documents that he believed, with a guileless innocence that belied his toughness, the authorities would allow to be published.

After Stringybark Creek, the gang disappeared from sight for several weeks, eluding the police parties that came in pursuit of them and using their highly developed bushmen's skills and the help of their friends in order to survive. Although Superintendent Nicolson, who was supervising the Kelly hunt from Benalla, had in place a network of spies and informers, none had yet yielded any results.

On 9 December 1879, the gang struck. Descending out of the Strathbogie Ranges, they commandeered the homestead at Younghusband Station, about five kilometres north of the township of Euroa. They bailed up anyone they could find on the station and locked them in the store shed. A visiting storekeeper called Gloster arrived with a cartload of goods to hawk at the station and was taken into custody, but only after an altercation that threatened to become violent. The four marauders then made free with the clothes and other items from his cart. The station manager, Macauley, turned up in the early evening and was also made a prisoner. The prisoners were kept overnight in the station's store, and the bushrangers took shifts to stand guard, allowing their captives out in small groups as a relief from the airless conditions. The women were left unmolested in the homestead. Early the next afternoon the numbers were swelled when a cart with four kangaroo hunters was apprehended outside the station. The cart was appropriated and the four occupants incarcerated.

The railway line to Euroa was nearby and the telegraph wires that were the township's link to the outside world ran beside the tracks. Leaving Byrne on guard at the station, the two Kellys and Hart took axes and demolished several telegraph poles and cut the wires. They were challenged by some railway workers who were forced to return to Younghusband and they too were placed under guard. The preparations for a raid on Euroa were now complete.

Byrne continued his role as gaoler as the other three set off for the town, Ned driving the storekeeper's covered cart, Dan the kangaroo hunters' open cart and Hart on horseback. Ned had with him a small cheque that he had forced Macauley to write. Steve Hart, whose identity as a gang member was not yet known, had visited the town two days earlier on a reconnaissance mission and the gang members had a carefully worked out plan of operation.

The National Bank was close to the railway station and had living quarters for the manager and his family attached. At a little after four o'clock, Ned went into the bank by the front door and Dan went around to the back. Hart remained on the street. They knew that the local constable and a fair number of the town's 300 or so inhabitants would be attending a court hearing some distance away. Ned did not immediately bail up the employee behind the counter. Instead he presented Macauley's cheque to be cashed and when the teller replied that it was not possible as it was outside of trading hours, Kelly produced a revolver and identified himself. The manager, Robert Scott, then made an appearance and was bailed up and forced to open the safe, where the robbers helped themselves to about 2000 pounds in cash and gold as well as two guns and some ammunition that had been supplied to the bank for use in such an emergency.

Ignoring Scott's objections, the robbers then went into the living quarters and rounded up Scott's wife, the couple's numerous progeny and a servant girl who, it later turned out, recognised Hart as a former acquaintance. They and the bank staff were loaded into the two carts and taken off to join the ever increasing throng at Younghusband Station. No-one dared give a hint of alarm to the few people they saw as they drove out of town. Now, with the telegraph down and the only witnesses to the crime in the gang's custody, no-one for the moment could raise the alarm.

Once back at Younghusband, Kelly released his prisoners into the open and Hart and Byrne treated them to a display of daredevil riding. That over, Ned turned to more serious matters, berating the assembled crowd with a catalogue of the injustices he, his family and his class had suffered at the hands of the squatters and the police, and pleading the case for his mother's release. Before leaving, he handed a bulky envelope to one of the women. It was to be forwarded to Donald Cameron, a member of the Victorian parliament whom Kelly thought might be sympathetic to his cause.

The letter was sent and a heavily censored version, designed to show the Kellys in the worst possible light and with all criticism of the police deleted, was later made public. Euroa had been a brilliant coup, but had failed to achieve its main objective.

New developments

The next few months produced a number of changes that affected the Kelly gang, both positively and negatively. Soon after the Euroa robbery, Superintendent Nicolson, the officer in charge of the hunt for the Kelly gang, instituted a witch-hunt in the Greta region, rounding up more than 30 known or suspected sympathisers of the Kellys. It was a heavy-handed and futile exercise that only served to reinforce sympathy for the Kellys and antagonism towards the police, especially since, as it was later admitted, Nicolson had no hard evidence against any of the people arrested, some of whom were held for as long as three months. All the suspects were eventually released without being charged, but only after a number of them had suffered serious financial hardship.

At about this time, too, Nicolson, who relied heavily on spies and informers, enlisted the help of Aaron Sherritt as a paid informer. The extent of Sherritt's treachery is uncertain. He certainly passed information to the police, but its reliability was often suspect and it was sometimes plainly inaccurate. He was still closely in touch with the families of his former friends and paid his attentions at different times after his contract with Nicolson to Byrne's sister, Catherine, and two of the Kelly girls: Maggie Skillion, whose husband was still in prison, and 16-year-old Kate. Suspicions, already aroused, must have seemed confirmed when, in July 1879, he was charged with stealing a horse from Catherine Byrne and giving it to Maggie Skillion. The charge was dismissed despite convincing evidence of his guilt. He was now, in the eyes of the Kellys and the Byrnes, clearly in league with the police. Less than 18 months later, he would pay with his life.

In March 1879, in a move that certainly put added pressure on the gang, six Aboriginal trackers under the command of a young Queenslander, Sub-Inspector Stanhope O'Connor, were brought in to help with the search.

In April 1879, partly because of the failed round-up, the chief commissioner of the Victorian police, Captain Standish, replaced Superintendent Nicolson with his longtime rival and antagonist, Superintendent Hare. Hare, a South African with a British Army background, was all for direct action and had little time for the intricacies of spy networks. He immediately instituted a series of forays, which he led himself, into the bush in futile attempts to flush out the gang. If he ever came near his quarry, they had prior warning of his approach.

Nicolson took over again in July and once more antagonised poor local farmers by recommending that suspected or known Kelly supporters be refused the right to select land.

Across the border

In the midst of all this furious activity, in February 1879, the Kellys pulled off another daring raid—not, as Sherritt had led the police to expect, on Goulburn, but more than 500 kilometres to the south-west on the New South Wales Riverina town of Jerilderie. As was the case in the Euroa raid, this one was brilliantly planned and perfectly executed. It managed to leave the local police looking absurdly inept, it both hoodwinked and entertained the local townsfolk, and it yielded the robbers another haul of more than 2000 pounds. It left no casualties except the pride of several policemen and the stocks of the local branch of the Bank of New South Wales.

Jerilderie, however, like Euroa, was a disappointment for Kelly. Once again he failed to get his message across. He went to the town armed, not only with weapons, but with an unwieldy 57-page document, laboriously written out in his own handwriting and setting out at even greater length than in his missive to the Victorian parliamentarian his defence, his grievances and his demands. It was by any literary standards ill-written and in places crudely abusive, but it was to be delivered to the editor of the local newspaper for publication. The 'Jerilderie letter', as it later came to be known, never reached its intended destination.

The Jerilderie operation began on Saturday 8 February with a late-night call at the police station. Ned knocked on the door in mock panic, calling out that there was a violent disturbance at Davidson's, one of the town's six hotels. When Senior Constable Devine and his assistant, Constable Richards, came to the door to answer the summons, they were swiftly overpowered by the four gang members and were handcuffed and placed in the cells. Devine's wife then appeared and was apprised of the identity of her visitors. She was then forced to prepare beds for the gang, who took it in turns to keep a watch on the cells.

At this stage Jerilderie had no churches. On Sunday mornings a visiting Catholic priest said mass at the courthouse and an Anglican minister conducted a service in another local hall. Mrs Devine always prepared the courthouse for mass. She made this known to her captors and, accompanied by Ned, was permitted to

The Kelly gang holds up the Jerilderie police station in February 1879.

perform her normal duties. No suspicions were aroused, either then or on the Sunday afternoon, when, dressed in borrowed police uniforms—white trousers, black jacket and black peaked cap—Ned and Byrne casually strolled through the town, accompanied by an overawed Constable Richards. Richards' revolver, emptied of its ammunition, was, as usual, in its holster. Visiting 'constables' Kelly and Byrne had loaded guns. The visitors, with the policeman as their guide, were familiarising themselves with the layout of the town and especially with the position and set-up of the town's only bank, the Bank of New South Wales. They were no doubt savouring the delicious irony of the situation.

Monday 10 February was to be the day of the hold-up, but first there was a practical matter to attend to. Early in the morning Byrne took two of the gang's horses to one of the town's two blacksmiths to have them shod. He told the accommodating smith to charge the service to the police account. Then, at about lunchtime, all four outlaws, disguised as police and still with Richards as hostage, held up the bar of the Royal Mail Hotel, adjacent to the bank, and demanded that the publican, whose name was Cox, provide drinks for the company. He then announced to the startled company his intention to rob the bank.

Ned Kelly and Byrne then went into the bank and obliged the teller and the accountant, Edwin Living, to join them next door in the hotel. The bank manager, Tarleton, was not in the bank, so Living took Ned into the living quarters where they disturbed him luxuriating in a warm bath. Being in no condition to resist, Tarleton provided the safe keys and, after dressing, was escorted next door. The bushrangers helped themselves to the contents of the safe and the teller's drawers, a total of more than 2000 pounds in notes and coins.

While ransacking the bank, Ned Kelly was annoyed to find a collection of mortgage deeds. These to him symbolised the bank's exploitation of struggling landholders and he was determined to destroy them. He was making a fire in the space behind the bank dwelling when he noticed three men slip out of the back of the hotel and run off. Kelly gave chase, caught one of the men and forced him at gunpoint back into the hotel. He then ascertained, to his great chagrin, that one of the escapees was the man he most wanted to confront—Gill, the editor of the local newspaper.

Kelly went to Gill's house and confronted his wife, who claimed not to know her husband's whereabouts—he was by now on his way to Deniliquin to alert the police—and who declined Kelly's invitation to deliver his document to her husband. Living promised to perform that service and Kelly left it with him. As the promise was given under duress, Living no doubt had no compunctions about not honouring it.

Kelly had to make do with a lengthy speech—a repeat of his Euroa performance—to his captive audience in the Royal Mail.

The mood of calm confidence and control that characterised most of the raid on Jerilderie turned ominously sour at one point and highlighted some of the tensions that had developed within the gang. In the Royal Mail, Hart was ill-at-ease and his manner had become aggressive and threatening. While Kelly was out of the hotel, Hart rudely snatched a gold watch from a clergyman, Mr Gribble. When Kelly heard of this affront he ordered Hart to return it, which he unwillingly did. Hart then demanded that Cox hand over his watch and got into an angry argument with Kelly when the latter again intervened to stop him. Kelly's authority prevailed when he told the younger man to 'Shut your mouth, you're nothing but a bloody thing'.

The young hooligan's mood improved enough soon afterwards for him to join Byrne in treating the largely admiring crowd to a valedictory display of spectacular horsmanship.

As at Euroa, the gang took the precaution of cutting down telegraph poles and cutting wires before riding out of town, each in a different direction. The police were left locked in their cells and the townsfolk instructed not to free them for at least three hours.

Glenrowan

It was to be another 16 months before the gang struck again, and when they did it was with an act of premeditated and cold-blooded murder that was at once a savage vendetta and part of a larger strategy that went disastrously wrong.

By this time the Kelly's plans had become grandiose, perhaps wildly so. A gang of four at the head of an army of small farmers that would wreak havoc across north-eastern Victoria, avenging the wrongs that had been visited on their class; a raid on the township of Glenrowan that would far outshine the brilliance of the Euroa and Jerilderie attacks and that would resonate throughout the colonies; a civil uprising, no less. The resonance is still felt today—the siege at Glenrowan joins the earlier Eureka Stockade uprising as one of the two most celebrated battles to have taken place on Australian soil—but the dream evaporated, along with the band of armed supporters who had turned out to help secure the victory, as three of the Kelly gang were gunned to death and their leader, his head and upper body clad in rough armour and looking like a grotesque parody of a mediaeval knight, was brought down by a hail of bullets to his unprotected legs as he courageously advanced to meet the encircling troopers. That image as much as anything else has fired the imagination of succeeding generations of Australians and has ensured the continuation of the Kelly legend.

Sherritt's execution for being a police informer—though his role has often been portrayed more as that of a police *mis*informer—was an integral part of the Glenrowan plan. Sherritt lived, with his wife, Ellen, and her mother, in a simple two-roomed hut at Woolshed, a little over 10 kilometres north-west of Beechworth. The gang members knew that he was guarded 24 hours a day by four police. This information would have been passed on to them by Byrne's mother and sister, who lived nearby, and on whom the police were also spying. The Kelly gang assumed, reasonably enough, that if Sherritt were killed, these policemen would quickly raise the alarm. The police at Beechworth would telegraph Benalla, the centre of local police operations, and a trainload of police—the police, as Kelly well knew, always used the railways, which helped explain their disadvantage when they were forced into the bush—would be hastily dispatched from Benalla to Beechworth, along the line that passed through Glenrowan. Glenrowan's advantage, from the Kelly's viewpoint, was that it was a town in decline. Until the railway came in 1873, it had been a modest township that served the nearby gold diggings, but the railway had seen it upstaged in favour of Benalla and Wangaratta. Its two hotels, general store and blacksmith's shop now served mainly the fruit-growing industry that had recently grown up there. The police would hardly expect an attack at such an out-of-the-way place.

The Kelly gang would commandeer Ann Jones's Glenrowan Inn, which was little more than a simple iron-roofed weatherboard hut with a verandah in front and a slab and bark dwelling at the rear, and which was adjacent to the Glenrowan railway platform. They would remove a section of the line on the Wangaratta side of the platform and would thus derail the police train just after it passed through Glenrowan, making it vulnerable to attack. The gang were dressed in protective armour that they had forged in an improvised bush forge from mouldboards and ploughshares purloined from, or willingly donated by, local farmers. They were supported by a group of as many as 800 armed supporters, and their plan was to battle it out with the police and take the survivors hostage.

That was the plan; the reality was very different. Sherritt's killing at least went to plan. Joe Byrne, his former friend, accomplished that. On the evening of Saturday 26 June 1880, he and Dan Kelly waited near Sherritt's dwelling and bailed up a German market gardener, Anton Wicks. They forced him to knock on the door under the pretence of asking directions. When Sherritt answered the door, after verifying the identity of the caller, he was met with a burst of gunfire from Byrne and staggered back into his hut, mortally wounded. After waiting some time at the hut, and observing no movement inside the hut, Byrne and Dan Kelly rode the 40 or so kilometres to meet up with Ned Kelly and Hart at Glenrowan. They arrived soon after dawn to find preparations for the battle well in hand.

Ned and Hart had already taken over Ann Jones's hotel and had begun rounding up anyone they could find in the township. Ned had also forced a gang of railway workers who were in the vicinity of the hotel to tear up a section of the railway line to the north of the Glenrowan platform. It was now almost 12 hours since Sherritt's murder and Kelly estimated that the expected train should not be long in arriving.

What he did not know is that the policeman at the Woolshed hut were still inside, paralysed with fear and not realising that Sherritt's assailants had left. About mid-morning one of them ventured sheepishly out and, finding that the coast was clear, had ridden in to Beechworth to break the news. It was almost three o'clock in the afternoon before word got to Benalla and Superintendent Hare, who had recently been reinstated as head of the Kelly hunt. Even then, Hare delayed further. He telegraphed to Melbourne to have O'Connor and his six Aboriginal trackers come to Benalla to join the expedition. By the time they had arrived and a group of police had been briefed, armed and boarded on a train, it was the early hours of Monday morning.

At the Glenrowan Inn about 60 people, now feeling weary and apprehensive, were held captive. In the hills

This 1894 painting by Patrick William Marony represents fairly accurately the details of the Kelly gang's armour

above the town, an unknown number of armed supporters were waiting with growing frustration for a prearranged signal to join the battle. A festive air had prevailed at the inn during much of Sunday as liberal amounts of liquor were consumed and music and dancing were improvised. The gang sensed little antipathy towards them. One of their prisoners, Thomas Curnow, the local schoolmaster, who had been bailed up with his wife and sister as he rode his buggy past the inn, had been particularly friendly and helpful. Curnow had informed Ned Kelly of the whereabouts of the local policeman, Constable Bracken, and had also warned him that the local stationmaster was in possession of a loaded gun.

As midnight passed, however, a sense of foreboding, aggravated by alcohol and lack of sleep, had descended on the gang. Kelly was on the verge of

The police prepare to approach Glenrowan Inn.

abandoning the siege and leaving. That was probably why, against the dictates of commonsense and the advice of his brother Dan, he acceded to Curnow's request to be allowed to take his wife and sister home. He was overheard to tell the departing young man not to 'dream too loud'.

Curnow had no thoughts of dreaming. Instead, he took the two women home and then set out on foot southwards along the railway line holding his sister's red scarf and a lantern. At about three o'clock as the police train approached Glenrowan he managed to flag it down and inform those on board that the Kelly gang was in the town.

As the people at the inn heard the train approaching, there was a scene of great confusion. As the gang clambered into their cumbersome suits of armour, Constable Bracken managed to escape and dash across to the station, where the train had pulled in. As he got there Hare and his eight policemen and O'Connor and his six trackers were beginning to disembark with their 17 horses. Also on the train were O'Connor's wife and sister, who had come along out of curiosity, and five newspaper reporters. Bracken informed Hare of the situation in the inn.

As the police advanced on the now darkened inn, everyone inside was lying on the floor. The four gang members came out on the verandah and firing began on both sides. Early in the encounter, Ned Kelly was hit in the left arm, and shortly after in the right foot as a bullet ripped through his big toe and came out at the ankle. Byrne was wounded in the calf, and he, Hart and Dan Kelly retreated back inside the inn, where bullets were ripping through the flimsy weatherboards.

Ann Jones's two children, 13-year-old Jack and 15-year-old Jane, were both wounded—Jack, mortally, in the stomach, and Jane, seriously but not fatally, in the head.

Ned, despite his wounds, managed to reach the back of the inn, where, armour and all, he mounted Byrne's horse and rode off to make contact with his supporters and let them know that the plan had gone awry. Superintendent Hare, meanwhile, had retreated to the railway station to have a bad wrist wound, probably from one of Ned Kelly's bullets, treated. He was taken back to Benalla by train, from where Superintendent Sadleir was dispatched to the battle with nine reinforcements. As Hare went south, Constable Bracken rode north to Wangaratta, where he alerted Sergeant Steele, who set out with five troopers.

By daybreak there were more than 30 police forming a semicircle around the hotel and exchanging fire with the bushrangers. Sergeant Steele, who had worked himself into a frenzy, was firing wildly at the building and was only stopped by a threat from one of his own constables. Groups of prisoners had contrived to escape during the night, choosing to risk being shot in the crossfire rather than take their chances inside. One of them, Mrs Reardon, a railway worker's wife, clutched her baby as she ran. A bullet passed through the shawl in which it was wrapped, but narrowly missed the infant. Her 19-year-old son was less fortunate but lucky to survive. A police bullet hit him in the shoulder and ended up close to his heart.

Ned Kelly had managed to return and was inside when Joe Byrne received a devastating wound to the groin and fell, writhing in agony. Kelly watched him die,

Joe Byrne's body, propped up for photographers against the door of Benalla lock-up.

then stumbled outside, shooting at the police and eventually falling exhausted to the ground in the bush at the rear of the inn, out of range of the police guns. Meanwhile the battle raged on, between the police and the two remaining bushrangers.

As the daylight broke Ned Kelly summoned up new reserves of energy and stumbled back into the fray, a revolver in his right hand, his left arm awash with blood. He could no doubt have escaped, but returned to help free his two surviving accomplices. The police were amazed to see, for the first time in daylight, this grotesque figure, its head encased in a metal cylinder with only a narrow slit for the eyes and a coat draped over its heavy breastplate, advancing inexorably towards them. Bullets bounced off the armour, until two shots fired at Kelly's legs sent him reeling backwards.

Kelly was taken to the railway station where his wounds were tended by Dr

Nicholson, who had tended Constable Fitzpatrick's wrist wound after the incident at the Kellys' home more than two years earlier. Nicholson thought that Kelly would not survive and a Catholic priest, Father Matthew Gibney, who had come on the scene, administered the last rites.

By mid-morning all the remaining hostages, except one, an elderly man called Martin Cherry, who had been shot in the stomach and who would die soon after from his wound, were allowed to leave the inn. Sadleir, frustrated by the continuing resistance, decided to destroy the building and telegraphed to Melbourne to send a cannon. By mid-afternoon, however, shooting from inside had ceased and Sadleir determined instead to burn it down. One of the police approached cautiously with bales of straw and a can of kerosene and set it alight.

Father Gibney remonstrated with Sadleir and, ignoring the policeman's commands, bravely sprinted into the burning building. A policeman followed the priest and together they managed to drag out Byrne's now stiffened body and carry out the dying Cherry. Hart and Dan Kelly were found lying dead—apparently they had suicided—in one of the rooms. Their charred remains were recovered only after the inn had burned to the ground. With this cataclysmic scene, almost a century of Australian bushranging came to an end.

Two days later, Byrne's lifeless body, like Dan Morgan's before him, was posed for photographers, propped up with ropes against the door of the Benalla lock-up.

The final scenes

Kelly recovered from his wounds and stood trial before Sir Redmond Barry on 28 October 1880 on a charge of murdering Constable Lonigan. The next day the jury returned a verdict of guilty and Redmond imposed a sentence of death.

Kelly said to the judge after his sentence had been pronounced, 'I will see you there, where I go'. Despite widespread appeals for mercy, Ned Kelly was hanged at Melbourne gaol on the morning of 11 November 1880. Barry survived him by less than a fortnight.

Kelly's body, like those of several bushrangers before him, suffered desecration after death. As though he were some freak of nature, his head was cut off and subjected to phrenological examination.

INDEX

Aboriginal people, 3, 5, 8, 23, 44, 60, 107
Aboriginal trackers, 23, 93, 104, 177, 181, 187
Ah Fook, 169
Aitcheson, 70
Armitage, Edward, 157
Arthur, Lieutenant Governor George, 15–18, *17*, 19, 23, 25, 36, 55
Atkins, George, 68
Balfour, Colonel, 22, 23
Baker, Edmund, 129
Baker, Mary Anne (Black Mary), 128–130, 134
Barnes, John, 92, 96
Barrow, 57
Barry, Sir Redmond, 107, 143, 167, 192
Batman, John, 22–24, *22*
Bayliss, Henry, 108, 109, 110
Baynes, William, 144, 145, 146
Bean family, 35, 36, 37, 38
Bennett, Graham, 143, 146, 147, 148
Bennett, Mary, 39
Berryman, Bill, 121, 124
Berryman, Joe, 121, 124
Bethune, Robert, 18
Bigge, Thomas, 41
Black Caesar, 2–3
Black Mary (Howe), 8–9
Black Mary (Ward), 128–130, 134
Blackwell, Mrs, 19
Blanche, 135
Bodenham, Thomas, 12
Bond, Edmond, 108
Booth, O'Hara, 31
Bow, John, 82, 83
Bowen, Constable, 146, 147
Bowen, Sir George, 156
Boxall, George, 71
Bracken, Constable, 188, 189, 190
Brady, Matthew, 15–24, *16*, 25, 36, 46, 58
Brisbane, Governor Thomas, 41
Britton, Fred, 130, 132
Brown, 5
Brown, Catherine (Kate), 78, 79, 82, 83, 84, 85

Brown, John, 78, 82, 83
Brown, 'Little', 12
Brunn, Ludwig, 140, 141, 142
Bryant, James, 24
Bugg, James, 129
Burke, Michael (Micky), 95, 98
Bushranging Act 1830, 44
Byrne, Catherine, 181, 186
Byrne, Joe, 173, 174, 175, 178–187, 189, 190, *191*
Caesar, John (Black Caesar), 2–3
Cameron, Donald, 180
Campbell, David, 99, 100
Cannibalism, 11–14
Canowindra, 96–97
Cappisotti, Giovanni, 135
Captain Melville *see* McCallum, Frank
Captain Moonlite *see* Scott, Andrew
Captain Thunderbolt *see* Ward, Frederick
Carcoar, 95–96
Carroll, John, 121, 124
Cash, Martin, 25–39, *37*, 56, 57
Charters, Dan, 80, 82, 85, 86
Charters, Patrick, 82
Cherry, Martin, 192
Childs, Major Joseph, 56, 57, 69
Chinese people, 72, 73, 114, 123, 169
Christie, Charles, 74–75
Christie, Frank *see* Gardiner, Frank
Christie, Lieutenant, 54
Churchley, Trooper, 112, 113
Churton, 13
Clark, Annie, 74–75
Clark, Frank *see* Gardiner, Frank
Clarke, Anne, 122
Clarke, James, 121, 122, 124
Clarke, John, 103, 119–126, *125*
Clarke, John (Snr), 121, 122
Clarke, Margaret, 122
Clarke, Mary, 121, 122, 123, 124
Clarke, Thomas, 103, 119–126, *122, 125*
Clifford, Eliza (Bessie), 26–29, 35, 36, 37
Cobham, Superintendent, 118
Cochlan, John, 136

Cockatoo Island, 54, 55, 75, 76, 122, 128, 130
Collins, Lieutenant Governor David, 4, *5*, 6
Condell, Sergeant James, 153, 154
Connell, Mary *see* Clarke, Mary
Connell, Patrick, 121, 123, 124
Connell, Thomas, 121, 123
Cowan, 23
Cowper, Mr, 47
Cox, 184
Cox, Thomas, 13
Curnow, Thomas, 188, 189
Curran, Paddy, 52, 58
Daley, John, 91
Daley, Patrick (Patsy), 91, 92, 93, 94
Dalton, Alexander, 12
Dargin, William, 93, 94, 104, 105
Darling, Governor Ralph, 41, *41*, 42, 44, 55
Davey, Lieutenant Governor Thomas, 6, 7, 8, 40
Davidson, Sub-inspector James, 105
Davis, 13
Davis, Edward (Jew-boy), 58–61
Dawson, Charles, 151, 152
Day, Edward, 61
De Clouet, John, 97
Delaney, 131
Devine, Mrs, 182
Devine, Senior Constable, 182
Dickenson, George, 92
Dobbyn, Dr, 118
Donleavy, John *see* Lynch, John
Donohue, Jack, 42–45, *45*, 46
Donovan, John, 67
Dry, Richard, 22, 23
Duff, John, 107
Dunleavy, James, 100, 101
Dunn, John, 90, 91, 100–105
Eugowra Rocks robbery, 80–81, 90, 91
Eureka gang, 67
Euroa raid, 179–180, 184, 185
Evans, Evan, 108, 114, 115
Evans, John, 115
Evans, Thomas, 108
Faithfull family, 103
Finegan, John, 67
Fitzpatrick, Constable Alexander, 165, 166, 167, 171,

175, 192
Fletcher, William, 121
Flooks, Thomas, 67
Fogg, William, 75, 76, 77, 85
Fordyce, Alexander, 80, 82, 83
Forestier Peninsula, 30, 31
Forster, William, 57
Franklin, Governor John, 36, 55
Frazers, 47, 48
Fuller, George, 107
Gardiner, Frank (Darkie), 72–86, 74, 84, 87, 89, 91, 93, 96, 106, 149, 152
German Bill, 108, 109
German Charley, 96
Gibney, Father Matthew, 192
Gilbert, Charles, 91
Gilbert, James, 91
Gilbert, Johnny, 72, 74, 77, 77, 82, 91, 92, 95, 96, 99–105
Gill, 184
Gipps, Governor George, 52
Glanville, Richard, 61
Glenrowan, 115, 185–192
Gloster, 179
Goldfields, 62–71, 75, 119–121
Gordon, James (Mount), 100, 101
Gould, 169
Graham, John, 61
Greenhill, Robert, 11, 12, 13
Gribble, Mr, 184
Hall, Ben, 72, 74, 78, 79, 80, 82, 87–105, 90, 104, 106, 107, 122, 149, 152, 153, 154, 155
Hall, Benjamin (Snr), 87–99
Hall, Eliza, 87
Hall, Senior Constable, 171
Hall, William, 82
Hare, Superintendent, 162, 181, 189, 190
Hart, Steve, 174, 175, 178, 179, 180, 184, 187, 189, 192
Haughey, Senior Constable, 96
Heriot, John, 111, 112
Hewitt, 79, 85
Hobart, 4, 6, 8, 11, 16, 18, 25, 27, 29, 32
Hogan, John, 132
Horsington, 79, 85
Horsley, Captain, 61
Hosie, Trooper William, 76, 77, 85, 91
Howe, Michael, 7–10, 15, 19

Hell's Gates, 10, 15
Hunter, Governor John, 3
Icely, Thomas, 95
Ireland, 47
Jackey Jackey *see* Westwood, William
Jeffries, Mark, 20, 21, 22, 24
Jerilderie raid, 182–185
Jones, 31–35, 37, 38, 39
Jones, Anne, 186, 187, 190
Jones, Jack, 190
Jones, Jane, 190
Kavanagh, 31–35, 37, 38, 39, 57
Keightley, Caroline, 98
Keightley, Henry, 98
Kelly, Alice, 167
Kelly, Annie, 169
Kelly, Constable, 103
Kelly, Dan, 165–167, 173, 174, 177–180, 186, 187, 189, 192
Kelly, Ellen, 161, 166–169, 171, 173, 175
Kelly gang, 139, 143, 165–192, 176, 183, 187
Kelly, Jim, 167–168, 171
Kelly, John (Red), 161, 168
Kelly, Kate, 173, 173, 181
Kelly, Ned, 1, 107, 115, 159, 161, 162, 165–192
Kennagh, Patrick, 124
Kennedy, Sergeant Michael, 175, 176, 177, 178
Kennelly, William (Bill Cornelius), 11, 12
Kerr, Charles, 36
Kilroy, George, 43
King, George, 171, 172
Lambing Flat, 72, 73, 75, 76, 92
Landregan, Kearns, 50, 51
Lang, John Dunmore, 150
Latrobe, Governor Charles, 64
Lemon, Richard, 5–6
Living, Edwin, 184
Lloyd, Jack, 161, 162
Lloyd, Tom, 161
Lonigan, Constable Thomas, 165, 175–178, 176, 192
Lowry, Fred, 94
Lynch, John, 46–51
Macarthur, John, 40
Macarthur, Mr, 54
McBean, Robert, 161–162
McCabe, James, 20
McCallum, Frank (Captain Melville), 65, 69–71, 80, 159

McCallum, Paddy, 156
McCarthy, Father Timothy, 98, 99, 101, 105
Macauley, 179, 180
McCormack, 169
McDonald, Claude, 145, 146
McDonald, Falconer, 145, 146
McDonald, James, 95
McGlede's farm, 146, 147
McGuire, John, 78, 80, 82, 83, 88, 89
McIntosh, William, 132
McIntryre, Constable Thomas, 175, 176, 177, 178
McIvor gold escort robbery, 67–68, 80
McLaughlin, James, 102
McLean, John, 111, 112
McLerie, Captain John, 73
McMahon, Charly *see* Morris, Charles
McNeil, 111
Maconochie, Captain Alexander, 56
McPherson, Ewen, 116
McPherson, James Alpin, 149–158, 150
McPherson, Mrs, 115
Macquarie, Governor Lachlan, 7, 9, 10, 40, 41
Macquarie Harbour, 10–11, 13, 15, 20, 24, 25
Maginnerty, Sergeant David, 112, 113
Maher, Constable, 155
Manns, Gilbert, 82, 83, 86
Manns, Henry, 82
Manwaring, Detective, 115
Marsden, Rev Samuel, 40, 44
Mason, Louisa, 134, 135
Mason, Robert, 134
Mason, Thomas, 134
Mather, John, 12
Melville, Captain *see* McCallum, Frank
Melville, George, 68
Middleton, Sergeant John, 76, 77, 78, 85
Monckton, William, 134
Moonlite, Captain *see* Scott, Andrew
Morgan, Daniel (Mad Dan), 106–118, 108, 111, 113, 115, 116, 117, 145, 146, 192
Morris, Charles, 151, 152

Mount Dromedary, 35, 36, 38
Mulhall, Constable John, 135, 136
Mulligan family, 47, 48-49
Munro, Mr, 132
Murphy, Jeremiah, 68
Murphy, John, 67, 68
Nelson, Frederick, 103
Nelson, Samuel, 103
Nesbitt, James, 143, 144, 146, 147
Newton, Jack, 74, 75
Nicholson, Dr John, 165, 192
Nicolson, Superintendent, 162, 169, 179, 181, 182
Norfolk Island, 3, 27, 39, 52, 55-57, 69, 159
Norton, John, 93, 94
Nott, 157
Oatlands, 27, 28, 33
O'Connell, John Bligh, 156, 157
O'Connor, Inspector Stanhope, 181, 187, 189
O'Grady, Constable, 121
O'Meally, John, 82, 91, 92, 93, 95, 96, 99, 100
O'Meally, Patrick, 91
O'Shea, John, 61
Owen, Corporal, 69
Owen, Mary, 107
Parkes, Sir Henry, 134
Parry, Sergeant, 101, *102*
Pearce, Alexander, 11, 12, 13, *14*
Pechey, Dr, 98
Peisley, John, 73, 76, 77, 78
Pentridge Prison, 69, 75, 143, 159, 161, 169
Petrie, John, 150
Phegan, John, 121
Port Arthur, 25, *26*, 29, 30, 31, 33, 38, 55
Pottinger, Sir Frederick, 78-79, 82, 83, 84, 89, 90-94, 149, 153, 154
Power, Harry, 159-164, *163*, *164*, 168, 169
Pratt, Thomas, 36, 37
President, The, 64, 71, 159, 171
Price, John, 29, 38, 39, 69, 159
Priest, John, 19, 23
Pugh, William, 9
Quinn, Jack, 168
Quinn, James, 161, 168
Quinn, Jimmy, 168
Quinn, Ellen *see* Kelly, Ellen

Reardon, Mrs, 190
Renton, 20
Reynolds, Charles, 128
Richards, Constable, 182, 183
Roberts, John, 107
Roberts, William, 70, 71
Robinson's Hotel, 97
Rogan, Thomas, 143, 147, 148
Rutherford, George, 116, 118
Sadleir, Superintendent, 174, 190, 192
Sanderson, Charles, 82, 83
Sarah Island, 10, 11
Scanlon, 5
Scanlon, Constable Michael, 175, 176, 177, 178
Scott, Andrew (Captain Moonlite), 139-148, *140*
Scott, Bill, 121, 125, 126
Scott, Robert, 180
Seymour, David, 156
Shelton, Richard, 168
Sherritt, Aaron, 174, 181, 182, 185-186, 187
Sherritt, Ellen, 185
Simpson, James, 140, 142
Skillion, Maggie, 167, 173, 181
Skillion, William, 167, 173
Smith, 46
Smith, Bill, 43
Smith, John *see* Morgan, Dan
Smyth, Sergeant Thomas, 114
Solomon, Meyer, 93, 94
Sorrell, Lieutenant Goveror William, 8, 9, 19, 40
Standish, Captain, 181
Stanley, Lord, 56
Steele, Sergeant, 190
Stephen, Chief Justice Alfred, 85, 105, 126
Stoddart, Mr, 34
Strickland, Josiah, 153, 154
Stringybark Creek, 174-178
Sturt, Charles, 44
Success, The, 64, *65*, 69, 71, 159, 160, 171
Sudds, 41
Tavenir, William, 135
Taylor, James, 80, 85
Taylor, Richard, 85
Telford, Robert, 116
Thompson, 41
Thompson, John, 132, 133
Thunderbolt *see* Ward, Frederick
Tibbs, 22

Towey, Trooper, 15
Travers, Matthew, 12
Troy, Bill, 75
Underwood, Will, 44
Vane, John, 95, 96, 98, 101, 105
Vincent, Isaac, 110
Walford, Mr, 133
Walker, Constable Alexander Binning, 136, *136*, 138
Walmesley, Jack, 44, 45
Walsh, Bridget, 78, 80, 85, 88, 89
Walsh, Ellen, 78, 89, 90
Walsh, John, 84
Wantabadgery seige, 143-146
Ward, Frederick (Captain Thunderbolt), 127-138, *128*, 139
Warner, 67
Watson, Samuel, 111, 112
Watt, Thomas, 89
Webber, Bill, 44, 45
Wedge, 23
Wentworth, W C, 44
Wernicke, Gus, 144, 146, 147
Westlick, 8
Westwood, William, 51-58, 53, 61
Whitehead, 6-7
Wicks, Anton, 186
Wild Scotchman *see* McPherson, James
Williams, Lieutenant, 23
Williams, Thomas, 144, 147, 148
Williamson, William, 167
Willis, 152, 157, 158
Wilson, 90
Wilson, George, 68
Winch, Superintendent, 115
Winstanley, 38
Woolpack Inn, 34-35
Worral, John, 9
Wright, Senior Constable, 126
Wright, Wild, 169, 171, 172, 173
Wynne, Sir Watkin, 125, *125*, 126

99, 100,

Index 195

Mount Dromedary, 35, 36, 38
Mulhall, Constable John, 135, 136
Mulligan family, 47, 48-49
Munro, Mr, 132
Murphy, Jeremiah, 68
Murphy, John, 67, 68
Nelson, Frederick, 103
Nelson, Samuel, 103
Nesbitt, James, 143, 144, 146, 147
Newton, Jack, 74, 75
Nicholson, Dr John, 165, 192
Nicolson, Superintendent, 162, 169, 179, 181, 182
Norfolk Island, 3, 27, 39, 52, 55-57, 69, 159
Norton, John, 93, 94
Nott, 157
Oatlands, 27, 28, 33
O'Connell, John Bligh, 156, 157
O'Connor, Inspector Stanhope, 181, 187, 189
O'Grady, Constable, 121
O'Meally, John, 82, 91, 92, 93, 95, 96, 99, 100
O'Meally, Patrick, 91
O'Shea, John, 61
Owen, Corporal, 69
Owen, Mary, 107
Parkes, Sir Henry, 134
Parry, Sergeant, 101, *102*
Pearce, Alexander, 11, 12, 13, *14*
Pechey, Dr, 98
Peisley, John, 73, 76, 77, 78
Pentridge Prison, 69, 75, 143, 159, 161, 169
Petrie, John, 150
Phegan, John, 121
Port Arthur, 25, *26*, 29, 30, 31, 33, 38, 55
Pottinger, Sir Frederick, 78-79, 82, 83, 84, 89, 90-94, 149, 153, 154
Power, Harry, 159-164, *163*, *164*, 168, 169
Pratt, Thomas, 36, 37
President, The, 64, 71, 159, 171
Price, John, 29, 38, 39, 69, 159
Priest, John, 19, 23
Pugh, William, 9
Quinn, Jack, 168
Quinn, James, 161, 168
Quinn, Jimmy, 168
Quinn, Ellen *see* Kelly, Ellen

Reardon, Mrs, 190
Renton, 20
Reynolds, Charles, 128
Richards, Constable, 182, 183
Roberts, John, 107
Roberts, William, 70, 71
Robinson's Hotel, 97
Rogan, Thomas, 143, 147, 148
Rutherford, George, 116, 118
Sadleir, Superintendent, 174, 190, 192
Sanderson, Charles, 82, 83
Sarah Island, 10, 11
Scanlon, 5
Scanlon, Constable Michael, 175, 176, 177, 178
Scott, Andrew (Captain Moonlite), 139-148, *140*
Scott, Bill, 121, 125, 126
Scott, Robert, 180
Seymour, David, 156
Shelton, Richard, 168
Sherritt, Aaron, 174, 181, 182, 185-186, 187
Sherritt, Ellen, 185
Simpson, James, 140, 142
Skillion, Maggie, 167, 173, 181
Skillion, William, 167, 173
Smith, 46
Smith, Bill, 43
Smith, John *see* Morgan, Dan
Smyth, Sergeant Thomas, 114
Solomon, Meyer, 93, 94
Sorrell, Lieutenant Goveror William, 8, 9, 19, 40
Standish, Captain, 181
Stanley, Lord, 56
Steele, Sergeant, 190
Stephen, Chief Justice Alfred, 85, 105, 126
Stoddart, Mr, 34
Strickland, Josiah, 153, 154
Stringybark Creek, 174-178
Sturt, Charles, 44
Success, The, 64, *65*, 69, 71, 159, 160, 171
Sudds, 41
Tavenir, William, 135
Taylor, James, 80, 85
Taylor, Richard, 85
Telford, Robert, 116
Thompson, 41
Thompson, John, 132, 133
Thunderbolt *see* Ward, Frederick
Tibbs, 22

Towey, Trooper, 153
Travers, Matthew, 12
Troy, Bill, 75
Underwood, Will, 44
Vane, John, 95, 96, 98, 99, 100, 101, 105
Vincent, Isaac, 110
Walford, Mr, 133
Walker, Constable Alexander Binning, 136, *136*, 138
Walmesley, Jack, 44, 45
Walsh, Bridget, 78, 80, 85, 88, 89
Walsh, Ellen, 78, 89, 90
Walsh, John, 84
Wantabadgery seige, 143-146
Ward, Frederick (Captain Thunderbolt), 127-138, *128*, *139*
Warner, 67
Watson, Samuel, 111, 112
Watt, Thomas, 89
Webber, Bill, 44, 45
Wedge, 23
Wentworth, W C, 44
Wernicke, Gus, 144, 146, 147
Westlick, 8
Westwood, William, 51-58, *53*, 61
Whitehead, 6-7
Wicks, Anton, 186
Wild Scotchman *see* McPherson, James
Williams, Lieutenant, 23
Williams, Thomas, 144, 147, 148
Williamson, William, 167
Willis, 152, 157, 158
Wilson, 90
Wilson, George, 68
Winch, Superintendent, 115
Winstanley, 38
Woolpack Inn, 34-35
Worral, John, 9
Wright, Senior Constable, 126
Wright, Wild, 169, 171, 172, 173
Wynne, Sir Watkin, 125, *125*, 126